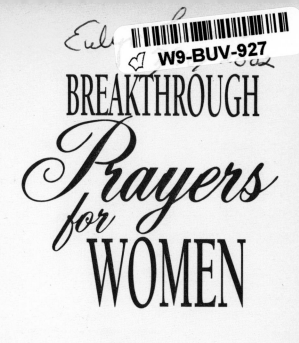

BREAKTHROUGH
Prayers
for
WOMEN

BREAKTHROUGH

Prayers

for

WOMEN

by
CLIFT & KATHLEEN
R I C H A R D S

Victory House, Inc.
Tulsa, Oklahoma

BREAKTHROUGH PRAYERS FOR WOMEN
Copyright © 2000 by K. & C. International, Inc.
ISBN 0-932081-70-3

Published by Victory House, Inc.
P.O. Box 700238
Tulsa, Oklahoma 74170
(918) 747-5009

Contents

PREFACE

The vision for this book began out of a deep desire to see women rise up to their fullest potential in Christ. To do this, we must become healed — emotionally, physically and spiritually. Prayer is the key to receiving. It is the divine connection to the One who created us and now holds us in the palm of His hand. God has a wonderful, divine plan for your life, and through the power of prayer, He will heal you, comfort you, and deliver you, helping you to reach your God-given potential.

Breakthrough Prayers for Women are not prayers to be simply read and recited. Pray these prayers like you have never prayed before — with power, passion, and persistence, knowing that He will do what you ask!

As you enter into prayer, let a new level of faith, authority, and expectancy come upon you, knowing that "He is able to do exceedingly abundantly above all that we ask or think, according to the power that works in us" (Eph. 3:20, NKJV). The power Paul mentions comes from the Holy Spirit who is working in *you*. Let His power come forth now, and accomplish great and mighty things in your life.

It's time for your *breakthrough!*

INTRODUCTION

How to Use This Book

Breakthrough Prayers for Women is not a prayer book in the traditional sense. It is not meant to be the only means of prayer for you to employ. Its style is very personal, and this enables you to apply the truths of God's Word to your prayer life and your life in general. This book will prove to be a tremendous aid to enable you to claim your rightful inheritance as a daughter of God, to reach out for all He has in store for you, and to get to know Him more fully.

The topical prayers of this book are built directly from the Scriptures. Because this is true, the book has a great variety of uses. The topics of the prayers are both personal and problem-centered; praying these prayers will help you make major breakthroughs in your personal life and spiritual growth. Therefore, one tremendous use of this book is for problem-solving regarding the issues of life you may be facing. The prayers of this book enable you to confront those issues in the power and authority of the Word of God.

With regard to the problem-centered approach of the prayers, counselors, teachers, pastors, friends, family members, and others can use this unique book to minister to a woman who may find herself enmeshed in particular difficulties. This will be possible because the prayers both teach and counsel through a process of prayer therapy that has been proven to have a multitude of positive consequences in the lives of individual women throughout the world.

You are about to discover that you can use and benefit from *Breakthrough Prayers for Women* in a multitude of other ways as well:

1. To gain greater faith.

2. To have your mind renewed.

3. To experience emotional healing.

4. To receive spiritual cleansing.

5. To receive the promises of God.

6. To grow in the grace and knowledge of the Lord Jesus Christ.

7. To be transformed.

8. To study to show yourself approved unto God.

9. To learn God's will.

10. To get answers to your prayers.

11. To find resolution for your problems.

12. To walk in truth, love, and confidence.

13. To trust God more fully.

14. To learn to hear God's voice.

15. To find full freedom and deliverance in God.

Admittedly, the above list provides only a partial look at the benefits you will derive from your use of *Breakthrough Prayers for Women*. Indeed, this book will revolutionize your life, give you greater confidence, and enable you to find a freedom you have never known before.

How the book can be used is further delineated in the following suggestions:

1. This is a personal prayer manual for you. It provides you with a practical means to begin, cultivate, and continue a dynamic prayer life that guarantees positive results in your life and the lives of others.

2. This is a fantastic tool for personal and group Bible study. Paul wrote, "Faith cometh by hearing, and hearing by the Word of God" (Rom. 10:17). This book will build your faith as you pray the Word, meditate upon the Word, and hear the Word.

3. This is a devotional/meditational guidebook that will greatly enrich your personal quiet times in God's presence.

4. This is an anointed tool to use in your personal work with other women as you counsel and share with them on a deeply personal level.

5. This is a topical reference work that is packed full of Scriptures and Bible promises which are extremely practical and personal, and may be used very effectively when you are teaching others.

6. This is a marvelous means for memorizing the Word of God. The Psalmist wrote, "Your word I have hidden in my heart, that I might not sin against You" (Ps. 119:11, NKJV). Memorizing God's Word will keep you from sin.

7. This is a personal reference work that will help you to grow in faith, trust God more fully, prevail in prayer, and ascertain God's will for your life.

8. This is a work of Bible meditation. Praying these prayers is a tremendous way for you to meditate upon God's Word, and this will lead to greater fruitfulness in your life, as the Psalmist declares. You will be ". . . like a tree planted by the rivers of water, that brings forth its fruit in its season" (Ps. 1:3, NKJV). He goes on to say that whatever you do shall prosper.

9. This is a life-changing giftbook that will keep on giving to women for generations to come.

10. This is a life-style book that shows you how to live as a liberated woman of faith in today's world.

As you use this book you will experience major breakthroughs in every area of your life. Not only will you find tremendous changes taking place in your own life, but you will also be an agent of change in your family, the church, the workplace, and the world.

Get ready for some life-changing, victorious breakthroughs as you use this book. By the time you're finished reading, you may not even be able to recognize yourself! Other people will wonder what happened to you, and they will want the same faith, hope, joy, love, boldness, and healing that you have acquired as a result of praying *Breakthrough Prayers for Women*.

SCRIPTURAL PRAYERS — SPIRITUAL BREAKTHROUGHS

And we desire that each one of you show the same diligence to the full assurance of hope until the end, that you do not become sluggish, but imitate those who through faith and patience inherit the promises. (Heb. 6:11-12, NKJV)

Personal Breakthroughs

A breakthrough is an act or point of breaking through an obstruction. In personal terms, this means breaking through the obstacles that may prevent you from moving forward in God, being healed, and finding the freedom God has provided for you through Jesus Christ. The topical prayers in this book enable you to act upon Bible-based faith in such a way that you will get totally beyond any and all obstructions in your way. Those obstructions (or roadblocks) may include doubt, fear, guilt, victimization, illness, as well as a host of other problems.

A breakthrough is an offensive thrust that penetrates and carries beyond a defensive line in warfare. It is active, aggressive, militant, bold, and assertive. This kind of breakthrough does not permit any kind of intimidation. It is this kind of militancy that will defeat the enemy in your life.

Breakthrough Prayers for Women will impart new faith and resolve to you which will enable you to fight "the good fight of faith" without fear or shame. Ultimate victory is yours already, and the prayers of this book will take you out of a defensive stance in spiritual warfare, into an offensive thrust that will cause the enemy to flee. (See James 4:7.)

A breakthrough is a sudden advance in knowledge or technique. The scriptural prayers of this book will help you to move ahead, to make major advances in your knowledge of God, your faith, your life, and your view of yourself and others. Through this book you will find freedom, success, and great advancement in the Kingdom of God.

Praying the Scriptures

Some might challenge, "What advantage is there for a woman to pray the prayers that are written down in this book?" The answer is simple and direct — these prayers provide a woman with a solid foundation of faith-filled, Scripture-based prayers so that her prayer life will become much richer and fuller than ever before, and she will have greater power to achieve true spiritual breakthroughs in her life.

The topical prayers of this book are written specifically for today's woman. They are built directly from the Scriptures for you (based on thousands of hours of prayer and research). The result is the astonishing power of these prayers.

Breakthrough Prayers for Women will enhance your prayer life in ways you never imagined possible. It will increase your faith and confidence, enabling you to reach out and receive all God has for you, which is far more than you presently may realize.

The key Scripture for this book is found in 1 John 5:14-15: "Now this is the confidence that we have in Him, that if we ask any thing according to His will, He hears us. And if we know that He hears us, whatever we ask, we know that we have the petitions we have asked of Him."

The prerequisites to power in prayer? Confidence in God. Asking according to His will. Believing that He hears your prayers. Receiving all He has for you. What a dynamic passage this is, and the following sections take a closer look at each of these prerequisites to personal breakthroughs.

Confidence in God

The topical prayers in _Breakthrough Prayers for Women_ are filled with faith and confidence in

God, your heavenly Father. This faith-filled confidence will enable you to trust God more fully. The Word proclaims, "Trust in the Lord with all your heart, and lean not on your own understanding; in all your ways acknowledge Him, and He shall direct your paths" (Prov. 3:5-6, NKJV).

To truly trust God means to take Him at His Word, in unwavering faith. Such devotion pleases the heart of your Father in heaven, as the writer of Hebrews declares, "Without faith it is impossible to please Him, for he who comes to God must believe that He is, and that He is a rewarder of those who diligently seek Him" (Heb. 11:6, NKJV).

The breakthrough prayers of this book are prayers firmly rooted in the soil of God's Word. They proclaim His promises very personally to your heart. They are nurtured in the sunshine of God's love, they are watered by His Word (see Eph. 5:26), and they are empowered by the Holy Spirit. (See Eph. 6:17.) Such prayers, therefore, will be extremely fruitful in your life, and by praying them, you will reap a rich and bountiful spiritual harvest. (See Ps. 1.)

Praying According to God's Will

How do you ascertain God's will for your life? The two most direct routes to this knowledge are prayer and God's Word. In fact, God's Word contains His will for your life. Therefore, when you pray His Word, you are praying His will, and the Scripture says, ". . . if we ask anything according to His will [His Word], He hears us" (1 John 5:14, NKJV). That's why praying the Scriptures is such an important practice for you to follow, especially if you want to see major breakthroughs in every area of your life.

Jesus said, "If you abide in Me, and My words abide in you, you will ask what you desire, and it shall be done for you" (John 15:7, NKJV). This is a clear personal promise for you to claim, and it comes directly from the lips of our Savior and Lord, Jesus Christ. Constantly abiding in Jesus, and letting His words abide in you, are keys to answered prayer.

Breakthrough Prayers for Women is focused very closely on the multitude of promises contained within the pages of the Bible. These promises are just as applicable for today's woman as they were for women in Bible times. Praying and personalizing the promises, as the topical prayers in this book direct you to do, will completely revolutionize the way you pray, think, view yourself, view others, and view God. This revolutionary approach to prayer will help you to realize more fully the truth that God declares: "You have seen well, for I am ready to perform My word" (Jer. 1:12, NKJV).

Yes, God is ready to perform His Word in your life today, and the breakthrough prayers of this book will help to set that process in motion, because: "All the promises of God in Him are Yes, and in Him Amen, to the glory of God through us" (2 Cor. 1:20, NKJV).

Here is one Bible promise for you to claim as you begin your work with this book: "The eyes of the Lord are on the righteous, and His ears are open to their cry" (Ps. 34:15, NKJV). Pray this truth, meditate upon its reality, believe it with all your heart, and act upon it!

God Hears You

Our Father's ears are tuned to the faith channel. His eyes are upon you, and His ears are open to your cry. He always receives your prayers of faith, based on the truths and promises of His Word, as loud and clear signals from your heart to His. Without faith, however, the signal of prayer is too weak for Him to hear; therefore, He cannot act upon it.

In order to develop the kind of faith that results in prayers that God will hear, we need to tune into His glorious Word. Paul wrote, "So then faith comes by hearing, and hearing by the word of God" (Rom. 10:17, NKJV). The dynamic faith signals that emanate from the Word of God give amazing power to your prayers as you appropriate His Word, through faith, for your own life.

Notice how this power works out in your life today: "Now to Him who is able to do exceedingly abundantly above all that we ask or think, according to the power that works in us" (Eph. 3:20, NKJV). When the power of God's Word is working in your heart as you pray, unlimited power is unleashed to enable you to receive all that God has for you. Paul writes, "And take the helmet of salvation, and the sword of the Spirit, which is the word of God; praying always with all prayer and supplication in the Spirit" (Eph. 6:17-18, NKJV).

God is able to do anything in answer to your prayers, but He needs your faith-filled cooperation to bring it to pass. Jesus said, "With God all things are possible" (Matt. 19:26, NKJV). Absolutely nothing is too hard for God. This confidence comes from knowing God's Word and incorporating its truths into your prayers. These are the kinds of prayers God is waiting to hear.

Whatever You Ask

Pray with confidence. Pray according to God's will (His Word). Pray with faith. These are keys to prayer-breakthroughs that will get you over life's hurdles, defeat the enemy, and permit you to make major advancements in spiritual growth and successful living. The Bible promises, "And if we know that He hears us, whatever we ask, we know that we have the petitions that we have asked of Him" (1 John 5:15, NKJV).

The important phrase, "Whatever [things] we [you] ask," is found several times in the Scriptures in connection with prayer. Jesus proclaims, "Assuredly, I say to you, if you have faith and do not doubt, you will not only do what was done to the fig tree, but also if you say to this mountain, 'Be removed and be cast into the sea,' it will be done. And whatever things you ask in prayer, believing, you will receive" (Matt. 21:21-22, NKJV).

You will receive! The key, once again, is believing faith. This kind of faith results in spiritual authority and prevailing power in prayer. Notice these words of Jesus: "Assuredly, I say to you, whatever you bind on earth will be bound in heaven, and whatever you loose on earth will be loosed in heaven" (Matt. 18:18, NKJV). Both in this passage and the preceding one Jesus opens His statement with the word *assuredly*, and this means, "You can count on it!"

Jesus loved to pray, and He was very much concerned that each of His followers would learn to pray effectively as well. To simplify matters, He developed a three-step process for you to follow in prayer: "Whatever things you ask when you pray, believe that you receive them, and you will have them" (Mark 11:24, NKJV). Ask, believe, receive. This is a formula to follow in all your prayers, and be sure that you don't leave out the receiving part. You receive by faith.

The Holy Spirit guides you into all truth, including truth about prayer. (See John 16:13.) He guides you, leads you, and reveals truth to you. He gives you important insights into the Word of God and the will of God. He is your teacher, helper, counselor, and friend. He promises to guide you, and He definitely will.

The general will of God is revealed to you in the Scriptures. This is known in Greek as the _logos_. His specific will for you is revealed to you through the Holy Spirit, and this is known in Greek as the _rhema_. You are able to ascertain both His general will and His specific will through the Scriptures inspired by the Holy Spirit, and through prayer in the Spirit.

Once you know both areas of His will for you, you are ready to act on your faith with certainty and confidence — the kind of certainty and confidence that brings results. Remember, all of the prayer promises in the Word of God are contingent on the faith that comes from knowing God's Word (and His will). In so doing you line up your desires with God's desires for you, and His promise is fulfilled in your life: "Trust in the Lord, and do good; dwell in the land, and feed on His faithfulness. Delight yourself also in the Lord, and He shall give you the desires of your heart. Commit your way to the Lord, trust also in Him, and He shall bring it to pass" (Ps. 37:3-4, NKJV).

As you trust in the Lord God, and do good, delighting in Him and His Word, He will give you the desires of your heart. As you commit your way to the Lord, He will give you the personal breakthroughs you need.

Remember, all of these prayer promises are contingent on the faith that comes from knowing God's Word. This is what enables us to perceive His will for our lives. In order to receive, we must be in accord with God's will.

We Shall Receive

John Newton, the writer of the hymn "Amazing Grace," penned these lines about prayer: "Thou art coming to a King, large petitions with thee bring, for His grace and power are such, none can ever ask too much." Newton's poem is confirmed by Jesus Christ who said, "Ask, and it shall be given you; seek, and ye shall find; knock, and it shall be opened unto you" (Matt. 7:7).

If we don't ask, we surely won't receive, but Jesus declares, "Every one that asketh receiveth; and he that seeketh findeth" (Matt. 7:8). Believing prayer is receiving prayer. _Breakthrough Prayers for Women_ are believing prayers, based on the Word of God, so they are receiving prayers as well.

Charles Haddon Spurgeon wrote, "Prayers are heard in heaven very much in proportion to our faith. Little faith will get very great mercies, but great faith still greater." This is an echo of Jesus' words: "According to your faith be it unto you" (Matt. 9:29).

Jesus frequently stresses the correlation between believing and receiving in His sermons. For example, He said, "And all things, whatsoever ye shall ask in prayer, believing, ye shall receive" (Matt. 21:22).

The Power of God's Word

The Word of God is the sword of the Spirit. (See Eph. 6:17.) It is your offensive weapon in spiritual warfare. Jesus used the Word of God to defeat the enemy when He was tempted in the wilderness, and you can do the same. (See Luke 4.) The writer of the Book of Hebrews describes the Word of God as follows: "For the word of God is living and powerful, and sharper than any two-edged sword, piercing even to the division of soul and spirit, and of joints and marrow, and is a discerner of the thoughts and intents of the heart" (Heb. 4:12, NKJV).

God's Word is alive, and when you pray its precepts, new life is imparted to you. It is amazingly powerful; in fact, the Word of God is a dynamo that unleashes great power when we pray its truths. The Bible is also sharper than any two-edged sword, and it is able to pierce to the heart of any enemy, issue, or matter that is affecting your life. If you use this sword when you pray, demons have to flee, and you will learn to see yourself more clearly, because the Word will reveal to you the thoughts and intents of your own heart.

As pointed out earlier, the Word of God also imparts faith to your heart. As you pray its promises, your faith will be magnified so that you will see God as He really is — the Master and Creator of the universe who knows what you have need of even before you express it to Him. (See Matt. 6:8.)

Meditation on the Word

By praying the Scriptures you are meditating upon the Word of God as you pray, and this will make an amazing difference in your life. The Bible says you are blessed as you delight in the Word of God and meditate upon its precepts. (See Ps. 1:1-2.) *Breakthrough Prayers for Women* enables you to meditate upon the Word of God in a full and personal way, and this will result in greater fruitfulness in your life.

By meditating upon the Scriptures as you pray, several things will happen. You will become ". . . like a tree planted by the rivers of water, that brings forth its fruit in its season, whose leaf also shall not wither" (Ps. 1:3). God promises you that whatever you do will prosper. (See Ps. 1:3.)

For all these reasons, _Breakthrough Prayers for Women_ has been prepared for you. As you approach the book with the great excitement that comes from expectancy and anticipation, amazing things will happen in your life:

You will get to know God better.

Your prayer life, and your life in general, will be revolutionized in powerfully positive directions.

Your faith will be strengthened.

Your trust in God will grow.

Your will become a receiver — a promise-reaper.

Your prayers will be answered.

You will rise up and be counted as a woman of God, full of confidence.

You will be healed emotionally, physically, and spiritually.

You will find your freedom as a daughter of God.

You will see yourself as the handmaiden of the Lord.

Your relationship with God, and all others, will be strengthened.

You will become prosperous and fruitful in all your endeavors.

You will be able to walk in the fullness of God's will for your life.

You will experience a multitude of spiritual breakthroughs.

You will take your place as a princess in the royal Kingdom of God.

Based on the Word of God, these results are guaranteed, because they are all promises from God himself who loves you with a perfect love. (See 1 John 4:18-19.)

It's exciting to think of the major breakthroughs you are going to experience as you use this book to the greater glory of God and the greatest possible advantage in your life.

Indeed, scriptural prayers bring spiritual breakthroughs!

DAUGHTERS OF GOD — WOMEN OF WARFARE

No weapon formed against you shall prosper, and every tongue which rises against you in judgment you shall condemn. This is the heritage of the servants of the Lord, and their righteousness is from Me. (Isa. 54:17, NKJV)

Break Down the Walls!

It is not God's will for you to live in discouragement, defeat, darkness, despair, or demonic oppression. He has a plan and a purpose for your life. In fact, He says, "I know the thoughts that I think toward you, . . . thoughts of peace and not of evil, to give you a future and a hope" (Jer. 29:11, NKJV).

God thinks about you, and His thoughts are of peace, not evil, because He wants you to realize your fullest potential as His daughter. He goes on, "Then you will call upon Me and go and pray to Me, and I will listen to you. And you will seek Me and find Me, when you search for Me with all your heart" (Jer. 29:12-13, NKJV).

You are a princess in a royal kingdom, the daughter of the Creator of the universe, and He loves you with an everlasting love. God says, "Yes, I have loved you with an everlasting love; therefore with lovingkindness I have drawn you" (Jer. 31:3, NKJV). The Father's love for you is everlasting. By faith you can declare these breakthrough-words: "For I am persuaded that neither death nor life, nor angels nor principalities nor powers, nor things present nor things to come, nor height nor depth, nor any other created thing, shall be able to separate us from the love of God which is in Christ Jesus our Lord" (Rom. 8:38-39, NKJV).

God loves you, and He always wants the best for you. He wants you to be a conqueror, and as His daughter, you have a right to claim His promise, "Yet in all these things we are more than conquerors through Him who loved us" (Rom. 8:37, NKJV). You are more than a conqueror!

When U.S. President Ronald Reagan stood at the Berlin wall he commanded, "Mr. Gorbachev, tear down this wall!" The Soviet Union, seedbed of communism, was an enemy of the Free World, and with boldness and confidence, President Reagan confronted the enemy. In a voice so authoritative that it still rings in many minds, the president defied the enemy and ordered him to demolish the wall that had divided people for so long, denying them access to friends, families, and so many other things on the other side. In due time the wall came crashing down.

This is a good example to use in spiritual warfare as well. It is not God's will for you to be blocked by any walls that deny you full access to Him and the wonderful inheritance He has given to you. "I will be found by you, says the Lord, and I will bring you back from your captivity" (Jer. 29:14, NKJV).

Breakthroughs involve breaking down any walls that hold us back from receiving all that God has for us, and this inheritance which He wants you to enjoy is outlined in Ephesians 1: "Blessed be the God and Father of our Lord Jesus Christ, who has blessed us with every spiritual blessing in the heavenly places in Christ" (Eph. 1:3, NKJV).

The apostle then goes on to reveal what some of these spiritual blessings are (See Eph. 1:15-23):

1. God chose you in Christ.

2. He wants you to be holy and blameless before Him in love.

3. God has predestined you to be adopted into His family.

4. You are redeemed through the blood of Jesus Christ.

5. Your sins have been forgiven.

6. You have received the riches of His grace, including wisdom.

7. God has made known to you the mystery of His will.

Notice that these blessings are yours already, and then the Apostle Paul goes on to pray specifically for you in the following areas. Receive these blessings as you reflect upon his prayer. Claim them as promises that are for *you*:

1. Your eyes are being enlightened with understanding.

2. You will know the hope of God's calling.

3. You have received the riches of His glory (your rightful inheritance).

4. You have the exceeding greatness of God's power through faith.

5. His power is at work in your life.

6. The authority of Christ rests upon you.

All of these promises are contained in the first chapter of Ephesians — an inspiring passage that reveals many of God's plans and purposes for your life.

The Power of Praise

When Joshua fought the Battle of Jericho, he used praise as a powerful and formidable weapon against his enemies, a weapon he used in breaking down the walls that held him back from breaking through to victory. This same powerful weapon is available to you, and the prayers of this book show you how praise leads you to victory.

"So the people shouted when the priests blew the trumpets. And it happened when the people heard the sound of the trumpet, and the people shouted with a great shout, that the wall fell down flat" (Josh. 6:20, NKJV).

The walls that prevent you from moving on in God will fall flat as you learn to use the breakthrough prayers of this book to defeat the enemy. You will shout your praises to God, who always inhabits the praises of His people. "But You are holy, enthroned in the praises of Israel, our father trusted in You; they trusted, and You delivered them. They cried to You, and were delivered; they trusted in You, and were not ashamed" (Ps. 22:3-5, NKJV).

Praise will enable you to break through every wall as you trust your Father to move in your behalf. Your job is praise Him, trust Him, and to cry to Him, and He will deliver you. You will never need to be ashamed, because the Bible declares: "And those who know Your name will put their trust in You; for You, Lord, have not forsaken those who seek You" (Ps. 9:10, NKJV).

The commandment of God is clear: "Make a joyful shout to the Lord, all you lands! Serve the Lord with gladness; come before His presence with singing. Know that the Lord, He is God; it is He who has made us, and not we ourselves; we are His people and the sheep of His pasture. Enter into His gates with thanksgiving, and into His courts with praise. Be thankful to Him, and bless His name. For the Lord is good; His mercy is everlasting, and His truth endures to all generations" (Ps. 100:1-5, NKJV).

The Psalmist knew the power of praise. He writes, "O Lord, our Lord, how excellent is Your name in all the earth, who have set Your glory above the heavens! Out of the mouth of babes and nursing infants You have ordained strength, because of Your enemies, that You may silence the enemy and the avenger" (Ps. 8:1-2, NKJV).

Praise silences the enemy in your life, and it smashes through the walls he has erected to keep you from experiencing the abundant life which is your rightful inheritance, but it does far more than that; praise opens the gates so that you can experience the very fullness of God!

Jesus came to give you abundant life. The Word proclaims, "The thief does not come except to steal, and to kill, and to destroy. I have come that they may have life, and that they may have it more abundantly" (John 10:10, NKJV).

Abundant life is yours! *Breakthrough Prayers for Women* will lead you into a greater measure of abundance than you have ever known before.

As you pray, remember to praise God for all He has done and is doing in your life, and your experience will be like that of the Israelites who discovered the power of praise: "It shall come to pass, when they make a long blast with the ram's horn, and when you hear the sound of the trumpet, that all the people shall shout with a great shout; then the wall of the city will fall down flat. And the people shall go up every man straight before him" (Josh. 6:5, NKJV).

The Power of the Holy Spirit

The Psalmist writes, "For You will light my lamp; the Lord my God will enlighten my darkness. For by You I can run against a troop, by my God I can leap over a wall. As for God his way is perfect; the word of the Lord is proven; He is a shield to all who trust in Him. For who is God, except the Lord? And who is a rock, except our God? It is God who arms me with strength, and makes my way perfect. He makes my feet like the feet of the deer, and sets me on my high places. He teaches my hands to make war, so that my arms can bend a bow of bronze" (Ps. 18:28-34, NKJV).

The power to accomplish these feats of spiritual strength — the power to break through walls that may surround you — is found in the Holy Spirit. Through His strength you can leap over those walls. Notice what

Zechariah wrote: "This is the word of the Lord to Zerubbabel: 'Not by might nor by power, but by My Spirit" (Zech. 4:6, NKJV).

Paul echoes these words in Ephesians 6 (a chapter that shows us the importance of the armor of God in spiritual warfare): "Be strong in the Lord and in the power of His might" (Eph. 6:10, NKJV). Then the apostle goes on to describe the armor of God, and he commands you to ". . . put on the whole armor of God, that you may be able to stand against the wiles of the devil" (Eph. 6:11, NKJV). That armor includes the breastplate of righteousness, the preparation of the gospel of peace, the shield of faith, the helmet of salvation, and the sword of the Spirit (the Word of God). Some pieces of this armor protect you from the assaults of the enemy, while other pieces enable you to assault the devil. You are protected by the righteousness that God imparts to protect your heart, the helmet of salvation to protect your mind, and the shield of faith that quenches all of Satan's fiery darts. Praying the prayers in *Breakthrough Prayers for Women* will enable you to put on each piece of God's armor with care.

Three defensive weapons are at your disposal as well — the sword of the Spirit, prayer, and the power of the Holy Spirit. Notice how Paul describes each of these vital forces. "And take the helmet of salvation, and the sword of the Spirit, which is the word of God; praying always with all prayer and supplication in the Spirit" (Eph. 6:17-18, NKJV). Each of the prayers in *Breakthrough Prayers for Women* is mindful of these important tools in obtaining spiritual victory, and by praying these prayers you will discover what powerful tools they are.

Notice the important link between the Word, the Holy Spirit, and prayer. Truly, they are inseparable entities. Used together, they always lead to personal, spiritual breakthroughs. Praying the Word of God is anointed praying — praying that is anointed with the power of the Holy Spirit. The Holy Spirit inspired the Scriptures, and His breath continues to give life to every page.

Jesus said, "Behold, I send the Promise of My Father upon you; but tarry in the city of Jerusalem until you are endued with power from on high" (Luke 24:49). When the Holy Spirit came on the Day of Pentecost the disciples were filled with a power that they had never known. God had fulfilled His promise that, ". . . you shall receive power when the Holy Spirit has come upon you" (Acts 1:8, NKJV).

That same wonderful power is available to you when you ask the Holy Spirit to fill you. (See Eph. 5:18.) He will do so, and as He does, He will enable you to rise above the circumstances of life, to leap over the walls that confront you. "For our gospel did not come to you in word only, but also in power, and in the Holy Spirit, and in much assurance" (1 Thess. 1:5, NKJV).

The power, assurance, comfort, teaching, guidance, and wisdom of the Holy Spirit are available to you as a daughter of God.

Faith to Conquer Giants

"For the weapons of our warfare are not carnal but mighty in God for pulling down strongholds, casting down arguments and every high thing that exalts itself against the knowledge of God, bringing every thought into captivity to the obedience of Christ" (2 Cor. 10:4-5, NKJV).

You, as a royal princess in the family of God, can become a victorious warrior in Christ. Praying *Breakthrough Prayers for Women* will enable you to be strong in faith and to realize the truth of God's Word: "For whatever is born of God overcomes the world. And this is the victory that has overcome the world — our faith" (1 John 5:4, NKJV).

You are an overcomer. You are a victor. You are a winner. You are more than a conqueror. Use all the tools God has given to you — the Word of God, the shield of faith, the power of the Holy Spirit, the power of the blood of Jesus, the power and authority of the name of Jesus Christ, overcoming faith, and the power of prayer — to vanquish every enemy in your life and to tear down the walls erected by the enemy to block your progress in spiritual things.

This is what young David had to do as he confronted the giant Goliath. Remember, others didn't think he could possibly win the fight, because he was so small and inexperienced. He was also poorly equipped. David was an uneducated shepherd-boy, but he had something that no one else had — faith in God — and it emboldened him, and saw him through to victory.

He spoke God's Word with boldness in the face of his enemy: "This day the Lord will deliver you into my hand, and I will strike you and take your head from you . . . . Then all this assembly shall know that the Lord does not save with sword and spear; for the battle is the Lord's, and He will give you into our hands" (1 Sam. 17:46-47, NKJV).

This is the attitude that you will need to win the battles you face and to tear down the walls that surround you. *Breakthrough Prayers for Women* is your battle manual. God, your Father, loves you, and He will see you through.

As you use this book, let God arise, and your enemies will be scattered. (See Ps. 68:1.) You will not regret it, because you will find freedom, deliverance, victory, and healing on every page. It's time for you to experience God's breakthroughs in your life. The breakthroughs you need are only a prayer away!

1

ABANDONMENT

A Breakthrough Prayer for a Woman
Who Feels Abandoned

Key Scripture: *"Forsake me not, O Lord: O my God, be not far from me"* (Ps. 38:21).

Prayer: Heavenly Father, even though I sometimes feel abandoned, I know you will never forsake me, and you will never forget your promises to me.[1] O my God, as I come to you now in the name of Jesus Christ my Lord, I know that you will make haste to help me.[2] Though others have forsaken me, I know you will never forsake me nor leave me alone.[3] Thank you so much for always being there with me.[4] You love me and care for me. You will never abandon me. Thank you that you will never forsake me, O Lord, and that you are never far from me.[5]

I rejoice in the truth of your Word which assures me that you will never forsake your people for the sake of your great name.[6] Thank you, Father. I cling to your promise which tells me that you will not cast away the righteous, and you will not help evil doers.[7] I believe your Word, Father.

With your help, mighty God, I will be a strong woman of good courage. I will not fear nor be afraid, because I know you always go with me, and you will not leave me nor forsake me.[8] Thank you, Father.

Even when family members may forsake me, I know you will lift me up.[9] Throughout my life, O God, I've never seen you forsake the righteous.[10] This knowledge gives me great comfort and peace. Lord God, you are my Rock.[11] I know that you will never leave me comfortless, and that you will always come to me.[12] Thank you, Father.

Because of your Word, I know that I am not abandoned. I rejoice in this truth, and I actively receive and experience your loving presence now as I pray. I love you, Father, and I will bless your name forever.[13]

References: (1) Deuteronomy 4:31; (2) Psalms 71:12; (3) Hebrews 13:5; (4) Matthew 28:20; (5) Psalms 38:21; (6) 1 Samuel 12:22; (7) Job 8:20; (8) Deuteronomy 31:6; (9) Psalms 27:10; (10) Psalms 37:25; (11) Psalms 18:2; (12) John 14:18; (13) Psalms 34:1.

2

ABORTION

A Woman's Breakthrough Prayer of Personal Repentance, and an Intercessory Prayer for Others

Key Scripture: *"For you created my inmost being; you knit me together in my mother's womb. I praise you because I am fearfully and wonderfully made; your works are wonderful, I know that full well. My frame was not hidden from you when I was made in the secret place. When I was woven together in the depths of the earth, your eyes saw my unformed body. All the days ordained for me were written in your book before one of them came to be"* (Ps. 139:13-16, NIV).

Prayer: Wonderful God, I come to you as a wounded daughter, because I realize the truth of the Psalmist's words. As a believer, I now know that abortion is wrong, because you write the number of our days in your book before our births. I thank you for the realization that I am fearfully and wonderfully made.[1] Thank you, Father.

My sense of sin and guilt sometimes threatens to overwhelm me. I thank you, Father, for your promise that if I will confess my sins, you will forgive me and cleanse me from all unrighteousness.[2] Therefore, I ask you to forgive me and to cleanse me from this terrible sin. Please forgive me for ever believing that abortion is okay, and most especially forgive me for permitting my child(ren) to be aborted. I now understand, Lord God, that this was not your will for me or my child(ren). I express faith to you, Father, that you have forgiven me and cleansed me from the unrighteousness associated with the sin of abortion. I also forgive myself.

I now know the truth, dear God, and the truth has made me free.[3] Thank you, Father. Now I will take my stand against abortion wherever I go. Help me to lead others to the glorious liberty you've given to me[4] as I walk in the total and undeserved freedom from guilt that you've imparted to me through the blood of your Son, my Lord and Savior, Jesus Christ.[5] I pray for the unborn children of the world, Father, that their parents will take responsibility for these precious children whom you love and have created for very special purposes, and I ask you to grant repentance to the hearts of mothers everywhere.[6]

PRAYER My earnest prayer is that you, Lord God, will so move in the lives of people all over the world so that every knee will bow and every tongue will confess that Jesus is Lord, to your glory, Almighty God.[7]

You are my refuge, and I thank you that your everlasting arms are always under me, giving me support and lifting me up. Thank you for your promise that you will thrust out the enemy from before me.[8] There is no one like you, Father, because I know you are the shield of my help and you are the sword of all excellency.[9]

Protect all the unborn children, Father, and watch over them like a hen watches over her chicks.[10] I rejoice in the wisdom and forgiveness you've imparted to me. I thank you, Father, in the name of Jesus Christ my Lord.

References: *(1) Psalms 139:13-16; (2) 1 John 1:9; (3) John 8:32; (4) Romans 8:21; (5) Ephesians 1:7; (6) Acts 11:18; (7) Philippians 2:10-11; (8) Deuteronomy 33:27; (9) Deuteronomy 33:29; (10) Matthew 23:37.*

3

ADDICTIONS

A Breakthrough Prayer for a Woman
Who Needs Deliverance From Addictions

Key Scripture: *"Stand fast therefore in the liberty wherewith Christ hath made us free, and be not entangled again with the yoke of bondage"* (Gal. 5:1).

Prayer: Heavenly Father, my struggle with an addiction to _____ has caused great pain in my life as well as the lives of others. I know it is not your will for me to be addicted to anything. Therefore, Father, in the name of Jesus Christ my Lord, I ask you to deliver me and set me free from this addiction. I receive your release from its grip and power now, this moment, as I pray. I believe you have set me free from my addiction through Christ, my Deliverer. Thank you, Father.

Now I ask for the grace to be able to stand fast in the liberty that Christ has provided for me, and help me to never turn back to this addiction again.[1] Thank you for sending Jesus who preached the gospel to the poor, healed the broken-hearted, preached deliverance to the captives, and recovering of sight to the blind.[2] I praise you for delivering me from all addictions,[3] and setting me free.[4] Your promises of freedom, victory, and deliverance mean so much to me, Father, and I know they are all yes-promises in Christ.⁵ I also thank you for hearing my prayer,⁶ and answering me according to your Word.⁷

I especially want to thank you for your promise that you will set at liberty those who are bruised.⁸ My choices have left me broken and bruised, Father, and I ask you to heal the effects of addiction in my life and the lives of others.⁹ Bind up my broken heart,¹⁰ and heal my body and mind.¹¹

Keep me in the hollow of your hand, Father.¹² I take delight in being the apple of your eye.¹³ Give me the grace to always stand fast in the liberty by which you have set me free.¹⁴ With your help, I will walk in freedom from addictions forever.

References: *(1) Galatians 5:1; (2) Luke 4:18; (3) Psalms 59:1; (4) Zephaniah 2:7; (5) 2 Corinthians 1:20; (6) Jeremiah 33:3; (7) Matthew 7:7; (8) Luke 4:18; (9) Isaiah 53:5; (10) Isaiah 61:1; (11) Jeremiah 17:14; (12) John 10:28; (13) Deuteronomy 32:10; (14) Galatians 5:1.*

4

ADULTERY

*A Breakthrough Prayer of Repentance for a
Woman Who Has Committed Adultery*

Key Scripture: *"If we confess our sins, He is faithful
and just to forgive us our sins and to cleanse us
from all unrighteousness"* (1 John 1:9, NKJV).

Prayer: Lord God, thank you for your Word
which clearly shows me the difference
between right and wrong. I confess my sin of
adultery to you, and as I renounce it, I accept
your forgiveness and your cleansing in my
life.[1] Thank you, Father.

Your Word commands me not to commit
adultery,[2] and with your help, I will never do
so again. I thank you for your commandments,
Father, and I desire to obey you in all things.
Give me understanding, and I will keep your
law.[3] Teach me to do your will.[4] All that you
reveal to me, I know I must do.[5] I seek your
strength, Father.

With your help, I will not turn aside to the
right hand or to the left.[6] I will keep your
commandments as I walk in your ways and
reverence you with great awe.[7] Through your
grace, I will serve you, my Lord God, with all
my heart and with all my soul.[8]

Teach me to walk in all your ways.[9] I want always to keep your commandments, Father.[10] From this day forward, I will walk in the Spirit, knowing that by so doing I will not fulfill the lusts of the flesh.[11] Thank you, Father.

Help me to reverence and love my husband.[12] Thank you for him, Father. Enable me to be a true helpmeet to him.[13]

References: (1) 1 John 1:9; (2) Exodus 20:14; (3) Psalms 119:34; (4) Psalms 143:10; (5) Numbers 23:26; (6) Deuteronomy 5:32; (7) Deuteronomy 8:6; (8) Deuteronomy 10:12; (9) Deuteronomy 19:9; (10) Joshua 22:5; (11) Galatians 5:16; (12) Colossians 3:18; (13) Genesis 2:18.

5

ADULTERY

*A Breakthrough Prayer of Healing for a Woman
Who Has Been Victimized by Adultery*

Key Scripture: *"Heal me, O Lord, and I shall be
healed; save me, and I shall be saved"* (Jer. 17:14).

Prayer: Heavenly Father, I need your healing
touch.[1] My husband's adultery has broken my
heart, and I need healing for the pain, anger,
and betrayal that I feel. I know that you heal
the broken-hearted, and I ask you to bring
your healing to my soul, my mind, my
emotions, and my feelings.[2] My faith in you
keeps me strong,[3] and I know you are working
your purposes out in my life as well as the life
of my husband.[4] Thank you for this wonderful
assurance, Father.

As I wait before you, I believe you are
restoring my soul.[5] You are renewing my
strength.[6] Through you, I know that I have a
hope and a future. I know you want me to live
in peace, not evil. Therefore, I call upon you
and pray to you, knowing that you are listening
to me. As I seek you, Father, I know I will find
you, because I am truly searching for you with
all my heart.[7] Thank you for the comfort you
give to me now through your Holy Spirit,[8] and
I welcome the blessing of His presence with

me now. Let your Holy Spirit minister your healing grace to my heart.

I pray for your continual guidance and direction today, and in the days ahead. I know that it is important for me to walk in forgiveness.[9] By faith, I now forgive my husband, and I ask you to help me to continue daily to walk in the freedom that forgiving him brings to me.

I release my husband now into your care, dear Father, and I pray that your kingdom come, and your will be done in him in every way.[10]

References: *(1) Jeremiah 17:14; (2) Luke 4:18; (3) Matthew 9:22; (4) Romans 8:28; (5) Psalms 23:3; (6) 2 Corinthians 12:9; (7) Jeremiah 29:11-13; (8) John 14:16; (9) Luke 6:37; (10) Luke 11:2-4.*

6

ADVERSITY

*A Breakthrough Prayer for a Woman
Who Needs Strength in the Face of Adversity*

Key Scripture: *"We are perplexed, but not in despair; persecuted, but not forsaken; cast down, but not destroyed"* (2 Cor. 4:8-9).

Prayer: Lord God above, Maker of heaven and earth, I come to you now in the name of my Lord Jesus Christ, seeking the strength I need in order to endure the adversities of the present time. Help me to be like Paul and to confidently proclaim, "I am perplexed, but not in despair; persecuted, but not forsaken; cast down, but not destroyed."[1] I realize, Father, that such a statement is possible only through the strength you impart to me.

In fact, you are my strength and my song, and you have become my salvation, Father.[2] Your right hand, O Lord God, has become glorious in power.[3] Thank you for the power of your right hand in the midst of my adversity. Thank you, Father, for fighting the adversity I face for me.[4] Impart your joy to me, O God, because I know this is a source of great strength for me.[5]

Lord God, you are my strength and my shield.[6] You are my strength and song.[7] Your

ways are strength to me.[8]   Give me your
wisdom, and strengthen me.[9] I thank you for
your wisdom which is better than strength.[10]
In quietness and in confidence I trust you,
Father,[11] and I will trust in you forever, because
you are my everlasting strength.[12]

Lord God, because I know you, I know I
shall experience your strength[13] in the face of all
adversity.[14]   Thank you for making your
strength perfect in the face of my weakness
and adversity.[15]

References: *(1) 2 Corinthians 4:8-9; (2) Exodus
15:2; (3) Exodus 15:6; (4) Joshua 23:10; (5) Nehemiah
8:10; (6) Psalms 28:7; (7) Psalms 118:14; (8) Proverbs
10:29; (9) Ecclesiastes 7:19; (10) Ecclesiastes 9:16;
(11) Isaiah 30:15; (12) Isaiah 26:4; (13) Habakkuk
3:19; (14) Daniel 11:32; (15) 2 Corinthians 12:9.*

7

AGING

A Breakthrough Prayer for a Woman
Who Has Concerns About Aging

Key Scripture: *"I have been young, and now am old; yet have I not seen the righteous forsaken"* (Ps. 37:25).

Prayer: Heavenly Father, thank you for the certain knowledge I have that you are always faithful,[1] and you will never forsake me.[2] Thank you so much for all the promises of your Word.

I seek for wisdom, Lord, and I rejoice in your promise that when I ask for your wisdom you will impart it to me.[3] Thank you for giving me understanding as a result of the experiences of my life[4] and through the teachings of your Word.[5]

Help me to continue growing in the grace and knowledge of Jesus Christ.[6] I confess that Jesus Christ is Lord over everything in my life including growing older, and that you, O God, are working mightily in me to bring forth the good pleasure of your will.[7] Thank you, Father. I ask you, Lord God, to be a Restorer of my life, and a nourisher of my years.[8]

Thank you for feeding me with the sincere milk of your Word,[9] and for enabling me, as a grown woman, to partake of the strong meat of your truth.[10] Help me to walk in your Word and in your truth at all times, as I endeavor to walk in your love, because I know your perfect love casts out all fear from my life.[11] Thank you, Father.

As I deal with the issues of growing older, help me to resist the enemy, and his thoughts and suggestions at all times.[12] I want to know you better each and every day, and to please you in all that I do. Strengthen and quicken me by your Holy Spirit[13] so that I can experience the abundant life you have for me.[14] Protect me from all fear.[15] Dear Father, I ask that my later years would be more fruitful than my former years.[16] In Jesus' name I pray.[17]

References: *(1) Lamentations 3:23; (2) Hebrews 13:5; (3) James 1:5; (4) Job 12:12; (5) Proverbs 1:7; (6) 2 Peter 3:18; (7) Philippians 2:11,13; (8) Ruth 4:15; (9) 1 Peter 2:2; (10) Hebrews 5:14; (11) 1 John 4:18; (12) James 4:7; (13) Romans 8:11; (14) John 10:10; (15) Psalms 27:1; (16) Haggai 2:9; (17) John 16:24.*

8

ALCOHOLISM

*A Breakthrough Prayer for a Woman
Who Needs Deliverance From Alcoholism*

Key Scripture: *"Wine is a mocker, strong drink is a brawler, and whoever is led astray by it is not wise"* (Prov. 20:1, NKJV).

Prayer: Heavenly Father, I come to you in the name of Jesus Christ my Lord. I confess my sin and I repent of my addiction to alcohol. Please forgive me for falling prey to its power in my life. I acknowledge that I need your power[1] and your wisdom[2] to enable me to walk in freedom from wine and strong drink which have led me so far astray.[3] With your help, Lord God, I will walk in the Spirit so that I will never again fulfill the lusts of my flesh.[4]

Fill me with your Spirit now, Father, and release your mighty power within me.[5] Break the hold of alcohol addiction in my life forever. I know the power of your Spirit is a key to victory over alcohol in my life. I want to be spiritually minded at all times, Father, because I know that to be spiritually minded is life and peace for me, but to be carnally minded is death.[6]

As a woman under your leadership, heavenly Father, I declare my breakthrough, and I will stand fast in the liberty wherewith Christ has set me free, and I will never again be entangled with the yoke of bondage to alcohol.[7] I will walk in your truth, because I know that your truth will make me free.[8] I will resist all of the enemy's temptations, and I know he will flee from me.[9]

Without you, Lord God, I can do nothing,[10] but through Christ I can do all things for He strengthens me.[11] I can walk free from alcohol because Jesus is Lord over every temptation and even the power of alcoholism must bow its knee to Jesus.[12] Thank you, Father, for setting me free, and for keeping me safe from alcoholism through Christ my Deliverer.[13]

References: (1) Ephesians 1:19; (2) James 1:5; (3) Proverbs 20:1; (4) Galatians 5:16; (5) Ephesians 5:18; (6) Romans 8:6; (7) Galatians 5:1; (8) John 8:32; (9) James 4:7; (10) John 15:5; (11) Philippians 4:13; (12) Philippians 2:9-10; (13) Romans 11:26.

9

ALCOHOLISM

A Breakthrough Prayer for a Woman
Who Lives With an Alcoholic, and a Prayer of
Intercession for Her Alcoholic Loved One

Key Scripture: *"It* [alcohol] *biteth like a serpent,*
and stingeth like an adder" (Prov. 23:32).

Prayer: Thank you, Father, for your great love
which keeps me free from all fear.[1] In spite of
my loved one's addiction to alcohol, I am able to
walk in the peace you give so freely to me.[2]
Help my loved one to see that his/her addiction
to alcohol does indeed bite like a serpent and
sting like an adder.[3] Help him/her to understand
that alcohol is a mocker in his/her life, that it
leads to raging, and it is not wise.[4] Deliver
him/her from this horrible addiction that is
affecting our family in so many adverse ways.

Father, I ask that all fear, turmoil, strife,
and confusion be removed from me and my
household. Take away the deception that
makes my loved one think that alcohol is good
for him/her. Show him/her that it is time to
seek you.[5] Father, let the realization of your
goodness lead him/her to repentance.[6] Draw
him/her to yourself, Father,[7] and restore
him/her to all that you had originally planned

for his/her life. Restore to him/her, and our entire family, the years that the locust has eaten.[8]

Give me your wisdom, Father, in all my dealings with my alcoholic loved one.[9] Help me to walk in love[10] before him/her, and always to speak the truth in love to him/her.[11] Lead him/her to acknowledge the truth, because it is only in so doing that you will be able to deliver him/her.[12] Let the power and anointing of the Holy Spirit come upon him/her and break the oppressive yoke of alcohol off of him/her.[13]

Thank you for hearing and answering my prayer, O righteous Father, as I pray in the name of Jesus Christ my Lord.[14]

References: (1) 1 John 4:18; (2) John 14:27; (3) Proverbs 23:32; (4) Proverbs 20:1; (5) Amos 5:6; (6) Romans 2:4; (7) Song of Solomon 1:4; (8) Joel 2:25; (9) James 1:5; (10) Ephesians 5:2; (11) Ephesians 4:15; (12) John 8:32; (13) Isaiah 10:27; (14) John 16:23.

10

ANGER

A Breakthrough Prayer for a Woman
Who Wants to Learn How to Deal With Her Anger

Key Scripture: *"Cease from anger, and forsake wrath"* (Ps. 37:8).

Prayer: O God, I come to you in the name of Jesus asking you to show me how to cease from my anger and to forsake wrath.[1] Sometimes my anger threatens to get the best of me, and I know this is not your will for me. Help me to be slow to anger so as to appease strife rather than to stir it up.[2] In my relationships with others, help me always to turn the anger of others away with a soft answer.[3]

With your help, Father, I will turn away from all inappropriate anger,[4] because your Word teaches me that anger rests in the bosom of fools.[5] Lord God, help me to keep from being foolishly angry.

Thank you for showing me that my wrath cannot work your righteousness.[6] Therefore, I seek your help to enable me to be swift to hear, slow to speak, and slow to anger.[7] Help me to never let the sun go down upon my wrath,[8] but to deal with my anger in positive, productive ways at all times.

My own experience and your Word teach me, Father, that wrath is cruel, and anger is outrageous.[9] For these reasons, and many others, I seek to walk away from anger in my life.

You, heavenly Father, are the Healer of all my inner hurts, frustrations, and disappointments.[10] Because I know this to be true, I ask you to bind up all my wounds and to set me free from all hurts and frustrations that cause me to feel angry.[11] Please give me the wisdom I need to deal with my feelings of anger in constructive ways.[12] Thank you for all you are doing in my life, Father. Thank you for teaching me how to deal with my anger.

References: *(1) Psalms 37:8; (2) Proverbs 15:18; (3) Proverbs 15:1; (4) Proverbs 29:8; (5) Ecclesiastes 7:9; (6) James 1:20; (7) James 1:19; (8) Ephesians 4:26; (9) Proverbs 27:4; (10) Exodus 15:26; (11) Luke 4:18; (12) James 1:5.*

11

ANOREXIA NERVOSA AND BULIMIA

*A Breakthrough Prayer of Personal Healing
From Eating Disorders*

Key Scripture: *"Eat, that you may have strength
when you go on your way"* (1 Sam. 28:22, NKJV).

Prayer: Heavenly Father, I love you and I
know you love me. I believe it is not your will
for me to suffer from this disorder any longer.
Help me to follow your admonition to eat so
that I will have the strength I need to follow
you.[1] Teach me how to eat my bread with joy,[2]
because I know you always give me my daily
bread.[3] Father, thank you for supplying all of
my needs according to your riches in glory,
through Christ Jesus.[4]

Help me always to remember that it's not
what I consume that defiles me. Instead, it is
what I speak that does so.[5] Give me clear
insights, and let your discretion preserve me.[6]
I need your help in overcoming anorexia
nervosa and/or bulimia in my life, Father, and
I ask for your healing,[7] your direction,[8] your
wisdom,[9] your understanding,[10] and your
keeping power.[11] Let the power and deception
of all eating disorders be removed from my
life. Let their strongholds be broken now.[12] In
Christ, I believe that I have been set free. Help

me to stand fast in the liberty with which you have freed me so that I will never again be entangled with the yoke of bondage to any kind of eating disorder.[13]

Father, I believe you have accepted me and received me[14] as I am. Thank you for showing me that I don't have to be perfect in order to be accepted by you. My heart rejoices to realize that you commended your love toward me through Jesus Christ.[15] He is setting me totally free, and because I know this is true, I know I am free indeed![16]

I confess that Jesus Christ is Lord over every area of my life including my eating habits.[17] Thank you for Jesus Christ who heals me,[18] and for setting me free from all eating disorders.

References: *(1) 1 Samuel 28:22; (2) Ecclesiastes 9:7; (3) Matthew 6:11; (4) Philippians 4:19; (5) Matthew 15:11; (6) Proverbs 2:11; (7) Luke 4:40; (8) Psalms 143:8; (9) James 1:5; (10) Psalms 119:144; (11) Daniel 2:20; (12) 2 Corinthians 10:4; (13) Galatians 5:1; (14) Romans 6:23; (15) Romans 5:8; (16) John 8:32; (17) Philippians 2:11; (18) Acts 9:34.*

12

ANXIETY

A Woman's Breakthrough Prayer
for Relief From Anxiety

Key Scripture: *"Cast thy burden upon the Lord, and He shall sustain thee"* (Ps. 55:22).

Prayer: Heavenly Father, I come to you in the name of Jesus Christ my Lord. I admit that I worry too much, and I recognize that I need your help to enable me to overcome anxiety in my life. Therefore, I now cast all my burdens upon you, Father, and I thank you for the knowledge that you will sustain me.[1] Praise you, Lord God.

You are my God, and I will prepare a habitation within me for you. I exalt you, Most Holy One.[2] I pour out my heart before you, Father, because I know you are my refuge from all worry and anxiety.[3] With your help, I will not let my heart be troubled, and I will not let fear rule my life.[4]

Thank you for your peace which surpasses all understanding in my life.[5] I will let your peace rule in my heart and mind.[6] Thank you for your promise that you will keep me in perfect peace as I keep my mind focused on you, Father, and trust in you with all my heart.[7]

Thank you for your perfect love which casts out all worry, anxiety, and fear from my life.[8] I know the torment of fear, Father, but I rejoice in your Word which declares that you have given me your peace in a way that the world can never give. Therefore, I will not let my heart be troubled or afraid.[9]

Thank you for your invitation to cast all my worries and anxieties upon you, Father.[10] I do so now, and as I do so, I experience your love,[11] peace,[12] and joy.[13] Praise your holy name!

References: *(1) Psalms 55:22; (2) Exodus 15:2; (3) Psalms 62:8; (4) John 14:1; (5) Philippians 4:7; (6) Colossians 3:15; (7) Isaiah 26:3; (8) 1 John 4:18; (9) John 14:27; (10) 1 Peter 5:7; (11) John 3:16; (12) Ephesians 2:14; (13) Psalms 32:11.*

13

BACKSLIDDEN

A Breakthrough Prayer for a Woman
Who Is Backslidden

Key Scripture: *"Having begun in the Spirit, are you now being made perfect by the flesh?"* (Gal. 3:3, NKJV).

Prayer: Dear Heavenly Father, the fact that I have forsaken you gives me great shame.[1] I was deceived into thinking that, after beginning a walk in your Spirit, I could fall back upon the flesh.[2] Forgive me, dear God, as I repent of my backsliding. How I thank you that you are forgiving me as I confess my sin of backsliding to you, and you are cleansing me from all unrighteousness.[3]

Thank you for your correction in my life which I experienced as I forsook your ways.[4] Whereas I had turned my back on you, I now choose to turn my face toward you,[5] to seek you with all my heart,[6] and to follow you in all your ways.[7] Thank you for hearing my prayer.[8]

How well do I remember from whence I had fallen, and I fully repent.[9] I will walk before you, O God.[10] With your help, I will henceforth keep all your statutes, and do them, because I know you are the Lord who sanctifies me.[11] Thank you, Father.

From this point on, Father, I want to do your will, not mine.[12] I will continue in your Word so that I might be your true disciple.[13] I love you; therefore, I will keep your commandments.[14] As I keep your Word, Father, I know your love will be perfected in me.[15] Thank you for forgiving me of my backsliding, and for taking me into your fold.

I bow my knee to you, Father, and confess that Jesus Christ is my Lord, and I will serve you forever.[16] Now I know that I can walk in victory because greater is He that is in me than he that is in the world.[17] Hallelujah!

References: (1) Jeremiah 17:13; (2) Galatians 3:3; (3) 1 John 1:9; (4) Proverbs 15:10; (5) Jeremiah 32:33; (6) 1 Chronicles 28:9; (7) Psalms 128:1; (8) 1 John 5:14-15; (9) Revelation 2:5; (10) 1 Kings 9:4; (11) Leviticus 20:8; (12) Luke 22:42; (13) John 8:31; (14) John 14:15; (15) 1 John 2:5; (16) Philippians 2:9-10; (17) 1 John 4:4.

14

BARRENNESS

*A Breakthrough Prayer for a Barren Woman
Who Wants to Have a Child*

Key Scripture: *"He settles the barren woman in
her home as a happy mother of children. Praise the
Lord"* (Ps. 113:9, NIV).

Prayer: Heavenly Father, your Word imparts
faith to my heart.[1] Thank you for your Word
which tells me that all things work together for
good in my life, because I am called according
to your purpose.[2] Thank you, Father. I believe
that you are able to do exceedingly abundantly
beyond all I can ask or think, according to the
power that works within me.[3]

Because I believe your Word, I am able to
rest in your exceedingly great and precious
promises.[4] Your Word gives me many examples
of women who were miraculously blessed with
children even though they were formerly
considered to be barren.[5] I ask you now for a
baby, Father, and I know that you are able to
perform the same kind of miracle in my life that
you did for the barren women in the Bible. I am
encouraged when I remember that your Word
tells me that children are a heritage from you,
Lord, and that the fruit of the womb is a reward.[6]

Thank you for all that you are teaching me as I wait before you. Your way is perfect, O Lord.[7] You enable me to mount up with wings like an eagle as I wait before you.[8] As I trust in you with all my heart, leaning not unto my own understanding, and acknowledging you in all my ways, I know you are directing my paths.[9]

Lord God, I surrender my life to you. Take me and use me in whatever way is best for me. I submit to your Lordship in my life.[10] I cast all my cares upon you because I know you care for me.[11] All these things I pray in the name of Jesus Christ, my Lord.[12] Amen.

References: (1) Romans 10:17; (2) Romans 8:28; (3) Ephesians 3:20-21; (4) 2 Peter 1:4; (5) Genesis 18, 1 Samuel 1; (6) Psalms 127:3; (7) Psalms 18:30; (8) Isaiah 40:31; (9) Proverb 3:5-6; (10) Revelation 4:8; (11) 1 Peter 5:7; (12) John 15:16.

15

BATTERED WIFE

*A Breakthrough Prayer for a Woman
Whose Husband Has Abused Her*

Key Scripture: *"God is our refuge and strength, a
very present help in trouble. Therefore we will not
fear"* (Ps. 46:1-2, NKJV).

Prayer: O Lord God, I come to you now in the
mighty name of Jesus and I thank you for all
the promises of your Word. I ask you for
healing[1] and help[2] concerning the abuse I have
received at the hands of my husband. Teach
me[3] how to deal with his physical and emotional
mistreatment. In your Word I find hope.[4]

Give me your wisdom[5] and your
understanding,[6] Father, I pray. Deliver me
from my husband's abuse.[7] You, O Lord God,
are my refuge and my fortress. You are my
God, and I trust in you.[8] Because of this truth,
I will not be afraid for the terror by night, nor
for the arrow that flies by day.[9] Thank you for
giving your angels charge over me, to keep me
in all my ways.[10]

As your Word directs, I pray for my
husband even though he despitefully uses me
and persecutes me.[11] Praying for him helps
me, Father. Thank you for your great love
which keeps me from fearing him.[12] I bless my

husband, O Lord,[13] and I ask you to help me to forgive him,[14] honor him,[15] and help him.

Father, your Word declares that what I bind on earth is bound in heaven. Therefore, in the name of Jesus Christ, and by faith in your Word, and through the power of the Holy Spirit, I bind the spirit of violence and abuse that operates in my husband, and I ask you, Father, to break its hold and power over him and set him completely free from it.[16]

I ask you to capture the attention of my husband, to draw him to yourself. Help him to see that you sent your only begotten Son to set him free from his sins and save him.[17]

Heal me, O Lord, and I shall be healed; save me, and I shall be saved.[18] Thank you for sending Jesus to heal the broken-hearted, and to preach deliverance to the captives.[19] I receive your healing as I pray. Thank you, Father.

References: *(1) Isaiah 53:5; (2) Psalms 70:5; (3) Psalms 143:10; (4) Psalms 130:5; (5) James 1:5; (6) Psalms 119:34; (7) Judges 10:12; (8) Psalms 91:2; (9) Psalms 91:5; (10) Psalms 91:11; (11) Matthew 5:44; (12) 1 John 4:18; (13) Romans 12:14; (14) Ephesians 4:32; (15) Ephesians 5:22; (16) Matthew 16:19; (17) John 3:16; (18) Jeremiah 17:14; (19) Luke 4:18.*

16

BITTERNESS

*A Breakthrough Prayer for a Woman Who
Wants Freedom From Bitterness in Her Life*

Key Scripture: *"The heart knoweth his own
bitterness"* (Prov. 14:10).

Prayer: Heavenly Father, my heart knows the
degree of bitterness I have allowed to creep
into my life.[1] I ask you, in the name of Jesus,[2]
to free me from all bitterness, because I realize
that a root of bitterness has sprung up in my
life, and its results involve defilement in my
own life and the lives of others.[3]

Forgive me for harboring bitterness,
Father, and cleanse me from all unrighteousness and bitterness as I pray.[4]

My bitterness has brought great anguish
to my soul, Lord God.[5] Father, I choose now to
forgive those who have offended or hurt me,[6]
and I ask you to bless them.[7]

I release to you all of my anger and resent-
ment over situations that I have become bitter
about by casting all of my cares upon you
because I know you care for me.[8] Heal me,[9]
and set me free.[10] I believe the promises of
your Word, and I accept the fact that Christ has
set me free. Therefore, I determine never again
to be entangled with the yoke of bitterness.

With your help, Father, I will stand fast in the liberty you've granted to me.[11]

I choose to work toward always walking in kindness, being tender-hearted, and forgiving, even as you have forgiven me for Christ's sake.[12] Hallelujah!

References: (1) Proverbs 14:10; (2) John 16:23; (3) Hebrews 12:15; (4) 1 John 1:9; (5) 2 Samuel 2:26; (6) Ephesians 4:32; (7) Matthew 5:44; (8) 1 Peter 5:7; (9) Isaiah 53:5; (10) John 8:32; (11) Galatians 5:1; (12) Ephesians 4:31-32.

17

BROKEN-HEARTEDNESS

*A Breakthrough Prayer of
Personal Healing From a Broken Heart*

Key Scripture: *"Is there no balm in Gilead? Is there no physician there?"* (Jer. 8:22).

Prayer: O God, sometimes I wonder if there is healing for my broken heart and all the hurts I've accumulated.[1] Your Word assures me, however, that you will bind up my wounds and your hands will make me whole.[2] Thank you, Father, for all the promises of your Word.

Help me to regain a merry heart, Lord God, because I know that a merry heart does one good, like a medicine, but a broken spirit dries the bones.[3] Through faith, I claim your promise that the stripes of Jesus Christ will bring healing to my broken heart.[4]

Heal me, O Lord, and I will be healed.[5] Thank you for the ongoing ministry of my Lord Jesus Christ whom you anointed to heal the broken-hearted and to proclaim deliverance to the captives.[6] I express faith to you, Father, and I receive your healing for my broken heart. Thank you.

Restore my soul.[7] Renew my strength as I wait upon you.[8] Help me to fully believe and to claim your promise that the old things are passed away, and you are making all things new in my life.[9] Father, with your aid, I will walk in wholeness and renewal from this time forward. Thank you for all that you've done for me.

Show me how to forgive those who have hurt me, Father.[10] Through your grace, I will walk in love and forgiveness toward them and all others.[11] Thank you for hearing and answering my prayer.

References: _(1) Jeremiah 8:22; (2) Job 5:18; (3) Proverbs 17:22; (4) Isaiah 53:5; (5) Jeremiah 17:14; (6) Luke 4:18; (7) Psalms 23:3; (8) Isaiah 40:31; (9) 2 Corinthians 5:17; (10) Matthew 6:14; (11) Ephesians 5:2._

18

BURDENS

A Breakthrough Prayer for a Woman
Who Feels Overburdened

Key Scripture: *"Come to Me, all you who labor and are heavy laden, and I will give you rest"* (Matt. 11:28, NKJV).

Prayer: Dear Father in heaven, thank you for your promise that, through Jesus, I can come to you when I feel overburdened, and you will give me rest.[1] I do so now, and I receive that wonderful gift of rest you have promised to me. Help me, Lord God, to walk in obedience,[2] faith,[3] trust,[4] and love,[5] so that I may be able to fully experience the rest you have for me.[6]

Father, I cast all of my burdens upon you, because I know you will sustain me.[7] I cast all my cares upon you, because I know you care for me.[8] I will not take back the cares and burdens I've given to you.

As I pour out my heart before you, I realize you are my everlasting refuge.[9] Thank you, Father. Through your grace, I will not let my heart be troubled, neither will I let it be afraid.[10] Realizing that the cares of this world choke out your Word in my life, with your help, Lord God, I will read and believe your

Word daily instead of giving heed to the pressures of this world.[11]

From now on, Father, I will seek peace and pursue it.[12] I will be strong in faith, giving glory to you, Father, for I am convinced that what you have promised you are able to perform.[13] I will imitate those who, through faith and patience, inherit the promises.[14] Thank you for enabling me to mount up with wings like an eagle, to run and not be weary, and to walk and not faint.[15]

References: (1) Matthew 11:28; (2) John 21:19; (3) Romans 10:17; (4) Proverbs 3:5-6; (5) Ephesians 5:2; (6) Hebrews 4; (7) Psalms 55:22; (8) 1 Peter 5:7; (9) Psalms 62:8; (10) John 14:27; (11) Matthew 13:22-23; (12) Psalms 34:14; (13) Romans 4:20-21; (14) Hebrews 6:12; (15) Isaiah 40:31.

19

BUSINESS

A Breakthrough Prayer for a Woman
Who Owns and Manages a Business

Key Scripture: *"The Lord shall make thee the head, and not the tail; and thou shalt be above only, and thou shalt not be beneath"* (Deut. 28:13).

Prayer: Heavenly Father, thank you for the business you've entrusted to me, and for all the promises of your Word which I claim and rely upon daily. I believe your promises of success, and I thank you for making me the head, not the tail, and for placing my business above, and not beneath.[1] I believe in you, Lord God, and I know you will establish me and my business as I serve you and obey your Word.[2] I thank you for the prosperity you've promised to me.[3]

I know you have the power to help me in all that I do.[4] Thank you, Father. As I continue to seek you, you continue to prosper me.[5] You are the God of heaven, and you are prospering my business.[6] Thank you, Lord God.

This business is your doing, Lord God, and it is marvelous in my eyes.[7] I commit my work unto you, along with the work of all my associates and employees, and I know you will continue to establish this business.[8] Help me always to remember, Father, that it is not by might, nor by power, but it is by your Spirit that this business will grow and be successful.[9]

Give me your wisdom, Lord God,[10] as I endeavor to manage this business as a faithful steward under your direction and blessing.[11] Father, you are the Chief Executive here, and I seek your continued blessing upon this business.

All things come from you, Father.[12] There is nothing better than to be able to rejoice in the work you've given for me to do.[13] The fact that you've given this business to me is an accomplished desire that is sweet to my soul.[14] Thank you, Father.

With your help, I will run this business to your glory,[15] my Lord and God, as I place my full trust in you without leaning unto my own understanding. In all my ways, Father, I will acknowledge you, and I know you will direct me in all my business affairs.[16] Thank you so much. All these things I pray in the name of my wonderful Lord, Jesus Christ.[17] Amen.

References: (1) Deuteronomy 28:13; (2) 2 Chronicles 20:20; (3) Deuteronomy 28:1-10; (4) 2 Chronicles 25:8; (5) 2 Chronicles 26:5; (6) Nehemiah 2:20; (7) Psalms 118:23; (8) Proverbs 16:3; (9) Zechariah 4:6; (10) James 1:5; (11) Psalms 25:4-5; (12) 1 Chronicles 29:14; (13) Deuteronomy 12:18; (14) Proverbs 13:19; (15) 1 Corinthians 10:31; (16) Proverbs 3:5-6; (17) John 15:16.

20

CANCER

*A Breakthrough Prayer of Personal Healing
for a Woman Who Has Cancer*

Key Scripture: *"With his stripes we are healed"*
(Isa. 53:5).

Prayer: Heavenly Father, I thank you for all
the promises of your Word which proclaim
healing to those who are sick. Thank you for
healing me through the stripes of Jesus.[1] I
believe your hands will make me whole[2]
because this is the promise of your Word.

Father, I take great joy in your promise
that though the afflictions of the righteous may
be many, you will deliver me out of them all.[3]
Thank you, God, my Healer.[4]

Heal me of cancer, O Lord God, and I know
I will be healed.[5] Thank you for strengthening
me.[6] You are the Lord God who is healing me.[7]
As I reach out to touch the hem of the garment
of the Great Physician, Jesus Christ, I believe
He is making me whole.[8] I rejoice in your
promise that you will heal me of all my
diseases, including cancer.[9] Therefore, I bless
you with all my soul, and all that is within me
blesses your holy name, Father.[10]

With your help, I will endeavor to keep
my heart merry each day, because I know that
a merry heart does me good like a medicine.[11]

Thank you, Father. I will endeavor to walk in the joy you impart to me, because I know your joy is my strength.[12]

Deliver me from all fear, thoughts, and imaginations the devil would bring to torment me.[13] Through faith in your Word, I now bring every thought, and all imaginations unto the captivity of Christ.[14] In the authority of the name of Jesus Christ, I confront cancer and all related fears, resisting them through faith.[15]

Your Word imparts faith for healing to my heart.[16] I receive your Word, your strength, and I receive your healing now as I pray. I know that through Jesus I have been made whole.[17] Thank you, Father.

You have enabled me to have the faith I need to be healed.[18] I believe your healing power is working in me now. My prayer is a prayer of faith, and I know you are healing me through my prayer of faith.[19] I receive your health, strength, and healing as I pray now in the name of Jesus my Lord. Thank you, Father.

References: *(1) Isaiah 53:5; (2) Job 5:18; (3) Psalms 34:19; (4) Exodus 15:26; (5) Jeremiah 17:14; (6) Psalms 28:7; (7) Exodus 15:26; (8) Matthew 9:21; (9) Psalms 103:3; (10) Psalms 103:1; (11) Proverbs 17:22; (12) Nehemiah 8:10; (13) Joel 2:32; (14) 2 Corinthians 10:5; (15) Matthew 16:19; (16) Romans 10:17; (17) Acts 9:34; (18) Acts 14:9; (19) James 5:15.*

21

CHILDBIRTH

*A Breakthrough Prayer for a Woman Who
Is Facing Labor and Delivery*

Key Scripture: *"Children are an heritage of the
Lord: and the fruit of the womb is his reward"*
(Ps. 127:3).

Prayer: Heavenly Father, as I come to you now
in the name of Jesus, I thank you so much for
the child you are giving to me. I truly regard
this child as an inheritance of your love, a
reward from your hands.[1] Thank you, Father.
Now I ask that you will be with me during the
birthing process. Let your Holy Spirit abide
with me and my baby and minister your peace
and comfort during the entire labor and delivery
process, and afterward as well.[2] Keep me from
fear[3] and illness.[4] Help me to focus on you as I
go through labor and delivery, because I know
if I will keep my mind stayed on you and trust
you, you will keep me in perfect peace.[5] Thank
you for this promise from your Word, Father.

Protect the child I'm bringing forth. Help
him/her to be a wise child that will bring great
joy to me.[6] Already, this child has brought
happiness to me.[7] Thank you, Father. I ask
that the labor and delivery will go smoothly,
and that you will enable me to cope with the

pain.[8] Father, you are my strength,[9] and I know you will see me through each phase of the process.

Give the medical personnel your wisdom,[10] strength,[11] and peace.[12] I look forward to the precious gift you're bringing into my life, and, Father, I thank you that you are able to do exceeding, abundantly above all I can ask or think, according to your power that works within me.[13] Hallelujah!

References: (1) *Psalms 127:3;* (2) *John 14:16-17;* (3) *Psalms 27:1;* (4) *Jeremiah 17:14;* (5) *Isaiah 26:3;* (6) *Proverbs 23:24;* (7) *Proverbs 23:24;* (8) *Isaiah 53:5;* (9) *Habakkuk 3:19;* (10) *James 1:5;* (11) *Psalms 28:7;* (12) *Colossians 3:15;* (13) *Ephesians 3:20.*

22

CHILD-REARING

*A Breakthrough Prayer for a Mother Who
Wants to Be a More Effective Parent*

Key Scripture: *"Children are an heritage of the
Lord: and the fruit of the womb is His reward"*
(Ps. 127:3).

Prayer: Thank you, Father, for the children
you've blessed me with. I accept them and
love them as being an inheritance and a reward
from you.[1] What an honor it is for me to be
their mother.

I come to you now in the name of Jesus
and I ask you to help me to train up my children
in all your ways, Father. I know this is my
responsibility, and I know that as I do so, I can
always be certain that they will not depart
from your ways when they are older.[2] Thank
you, Father.

As a mother, there can be no greater joy
for me than to know that my children are
walking in your truth.[3] Help me to set a good
example for them by always walking in your
ways,[4] your love,[5] your wisdom,[6] your light,[7]
your faith,[8] and your Word.[9]

Your way is perfect, Father, and your
Word is tried.[10] Help me to teach your ways
and your Word to my children.[11] Give me the

grace I need, Lord God, to lay up your Word in my heart and in my soul, and I will teach your Word to my children by speaking of your truths every day. I will post your words in my house so that my days and the days of my children will be multiplied.[12]

As for me and my children, we will serve you, dear Father.[13] Thank you for enabling me to be a good mother to them. Continue to give me your wisdom[14] so that I can be the best mother possible.

References: *(1) Psalms 127:3; (2) Proverbs 22:6; (3) 3 John 4; (4) Deuteronomy 8:6; (5) Ephesians 5:2; (6) Ephesians 5:15; (7) Ephesians 5:8; (8) 2 Corinthians 5:7; (9) Psalms 119:105; (10) Psalms 18:30; (11) Deuteronomy 6:7; (12) Deuteronomy 11:18-21; (13) Joshua 24:15; (14) James 1:5.*

23

COMFORT

*A Breakthrough Prayer for a Woman
in Need of Personal Comfort*

Key Scripture: *"Thou, O Lord, are a shield for me;
my glory, and the lifter up of mine head"* (Ps. 3:3).

Prayer: Lord God, I come to you in the precious
name of Jesus and I thank you for being a
shield about me. I believe you are my glory,
and you are the One who lifts up my head.[1] I
seek your comforting presence in my life.

Thank you, Father, for making me to lie
down in green pastures and leading me beside
the still waters. I believe you are restoring my
soul as I pray to you.[2] Your rod and your staff
are giving me comfort.[3]

It gives me such wonderful assurance to
know that you will always be with me, even if
I'm passing through deep waters of difficulty
or despair. I know that the rivers of discomfort
will not overflow me, and the fires of tribulation
will not burn me.[4] You are the only source of
true comfort for me, Father,[5] and I receive your
comfort now with deep gratitude.

Your comfort is like a mother's comfort in
my life, Father.[6] You are my healing salve, and
you are my physician.[7] Your Word does great
good to me.[8] Your Spirit lifts me up.[9] Even in

my mourning, I am blessed, because I know you will comfort me.[10] Thank you, Father.

Thank you for the Holy Spirit, my Comforter, who abides with me forever, and gives me His comfort.[11] Thank you for the peace you've given to me.[12] You are enabling me to not let my heart be troubled or afraid.[13] Because I know your Son has overcome the world, I can be of good cheer.[14]

I will continue to look to you, Lord God, because you are the Father of mercies, and you are the God of all comfort.[15]

References: *(1) Psalms 3:3; (2) Psalms 23:2-3; (3) Psalms 23:4; (4) Isaiah 43:2; (5) 2 Corinthians 1:3; (6) Isaiah 66:13; (7) Jeremiah 8:22; (8) Micah 2:7; (9) Haggai 2:5; (10) Matthew 5:4; (11) John 14:16; (12) John 14:27; (13) John 14:1; (14) John 16:33; (15) 2 Corinthians 1:3.*

24

COMPASSION

A Breakthrough Prayer for a Woman Who
Wants to Have More Compassion for Others

Key Scripture: *"Remember them that are in bonds, as bound with them; and them which suffer adversity, as being yourselves also in the body"* (Heb. 13:3).

Prayer: Lord God above, I come to you in the wonderful name of Jesus and I ask you to help me to walk in compassion toward others at all times, to remember those who are experiencing hardship as if I were in the hardship with them.[1] Help me to have greater empathy and compassion for others.

You are such a gracious God, O Father. You are merciful, slow to anger, and of great kindness,[2] and I want to be like you. You are gracious, and full of compassion. You are slow to anger, and of great mercy.[3] Help me to develop these same qualities in my life, O God. I thank you for the fact that you are merciful and gracious, slow to anger, and plenteous in mercy,[4] and I believe you are working these same attributes into my life, Father. Thank you so much.

Help me to obey you by loving mercy, doing justly, and walking humbly with you.[5]

Give me every opportunity to show mercy and compassion to my fellow human beings.[6] Help me to never be oppressive in my dealings with others.[7] Father, it is my desire to pray for others,[8] and when I do, please let your love and compassion flow through me to them.[9] Thank you for Jesus who explained that when I show compassion toward others, I'm actually showing compassion toward Him.[10]

Through your grace, Father, I determine to comfort the feeble-minded, to support the weak, and to be patient toward all people.[11] I will walk in love,[12] be empathetic, and be courteous[13] toward all.

Thank you for helping me to become a more compassionate woman.

References: *(1) Hebrews 13:3; (2) Jonah 4:2; (3) Psalms 103:8; (4) Psalms 145:8; (5) Micah 6:8; (6) Zechariah 7:9; (7) Zechariah 7:10; (8) Ephesians 6:18; (9) Romans 5:5; (10) Matthew 25:40; (11) 1 Thessalonians 5:14; (12) Ephesians 5:2; (13) 1 Peter 3:8.*

25

CONDEMNATION

A Breakthrough Prayer for a Woman Who
Feels a Sense of Inadequacy and Condemnation

Key Scripture: *"There is therefore now no condemnation to those who are in Christ Jesus, who do not walk according to the flesh, but according to the Spirit"* (Rom. 8:1, NKJV).

Prayer: Lord God, thank you for your Word which proclaims that I can walk in freedom from condemnation as I learn to walk according to the Spirit.[1] I believe your Word, Father, and with your help, I will continue walking in the Spirit so that I will not fulfill the lusts of my flesh.[2]

Father, I thank you for Jesus, and because I believe on Him I know I am not condemned.[3] It is the devil who accuses,[4] lies,[5] deceives,[6] and confuses.[7] In the power of the Holy Spirit, and in the authority of the name of Jesus, I take my stand against the enemy, through faith, and I know he is fleeing from me.[8] Thank you, Lord God, for the blood of Jesus which cleanses me from all condemnation.[9]

Thank you, my mighty God, for setting me free from all feelings of condemnation. I know I'm free indeed because your truth has set me free.[10]

Thank you, Lord God, for the forgiveness you've given to me in Christ Jesus.[11] It is incredibly wonderful to realize that you have cleansed me from all unrighteousness.[12] Thank you for your grace, Father, which is greater than all my sin.[13]

With your help, dear Father, I will stand fast in the liberty you've given unto me. Help me to never again be entangled with any yoke of bondage, Father.[14]

I believe you love me, Lord God,[15] and I thank you for commending your love to me while I was yet a sinner.[16] Your perfect love casts out all fear and condemnation from my life forever.[17] Hallelujah!

References: *(1) Romans 8:1; (2) Galatians 5:16; (3) John 3:16-18; (4) Revelation 12:10; (5) John 8:44; (6) 2 John 7; (7) 1 Corinthians 14:33; (8) James 4:7; (9) 1 John 1:7; (10) John 8:32; (11) 1 John 1:7; (12) 1 John 1:9; (13) Ephesians 2:8-9; (14) Galatians 5:1; (15) John 3:16; (16) Romans 5:8; (17) 1 John 4:18.*

26

CONFIDENCE

*A Breakthrough Prayer for a Woman Who
Seeks Greater Confidence*

Key Scripture: " *I can do all things through Christ who strengthens me"* (Phil. 4:13, NKJV).

Prayer: Lord God, I come to you in the name of Jesus Christ and I thank you for showing me that self-confidence comes from having confidence in you. You have shown me that I can indeed do all things through Christ who strengthens me.[1] This is so wonderful to know.

Because the battle is always yours, O Lord God,[2] I have greater confidence to be strong, and of good courage. The confidence you impart to me enables me not to be dismayed or fearful.[3] Even though I might have to walk through the valley of the shadow of death, I will fear no evil, because I know you are with me, Father.[4]

Because of you, I am able to be of good courage, realizing that you are strengthening my heart. Lord God, all my hope is in you.[5] You alone are my rock and my salvation, and you are my defense, and this certain knowledge keeps me from ever being moved.[6] In you, O Lord God, do I put my trust,[7] because I know you are on my side. Therefore, I will not fear.[8] Thank you, Father.

   With you all things are possible,[9] and this fact of your Word imparts great confidence to me. Thank you, Father, for not giving me a spirit of fear. Instead, you have given me a spirit of power, love, and a sound mind.[10] Thank you so much. Because of all these truths I will not cast away my confidence.[11]

   As I've prayed, Father, I've felt my confidence restored. I gladly lift up my hands unto you,[12] for you are my Helper, and I have no reason to fear anyone or anything.[13]   I believe and I proclaim that greater are you, O God, who is in me than he that is in the world.[14]

References: (1) Philippians 4:13; (2) 1 Samuel 17:47; (3) 1 Chronicles 22:13; (4) Psalms 23:4; (5) Psalms 31:24; (6) Psalms 62:6; (7) Psalms 71:1; (8) Psalms 118:6; (9) Matthew 19:26; (10) 2 Timothy 1:7; (11) Hebrews 10:35; (12) Hebrews 12:12; (13) Hebrews 13:6; (14) 1 John 4:4.

27

CONTENTMENT

*A Breakthrough Prayer for a Woman Who
Wants a Greater Sense of Contentment*

Key Scripture: *"Godliness with contentment is great gain"* (1 Tim. 6:6).

Prayer: Lord God, thank you for the gift of godliness which I realize is great gain for me.[1] Yet, sometimes, I don't feel content. Help me to experience a greater sense of contentment in my life.

Father, supply me with the things that are my true needs.[2] I thank you for always supplying all of my needs according to your riches in glory through Christ Jesus.[3] I feel great contentment from your promise that your blessing gives one a rich and full supply, and you add no sorrow with it.[4] Thank you for giving me peace with you through my Lord Jesus Christ.[5]

Teach me, Father, to be content with such things as I have,[6] instead of always feeling discontented and wanting more. Help me to learn, as Paul did, to be content in whatever state I find myself.[7] I know, Father, that it would be much better to have just a little when I'm walking with you, than to have great treasure along with great trouble.[8]

With your help, I want my eye to be satisfied with what it sees, and my ear to be satisfied with what it hears.[9] Having food and clothing, and all the other blessings you give to me, I will be content.[10] My heart rejoices in you, O Lord God.[11]

I put my trust in you, Father, and I have great joy.[12] Thank you for the awesome promise you've given to me — that goodness and mercy shall follow me all the days of my life, and I will dwell in your house forever.[13] These wonderful promises give me a full sense of contentment indeed. In Jesus name I pray, Father.[14] Amen.

References: (1) 1 Timothy 6:6; (2) Proverbs 30:8; (3) Philippians 4:19; (4) Proverbs 10:22; (5) Romans 5:1; (6) Hebrews 13:5; (7) Philippians 4:11; (8) Proverbs 15:16; (9) Ecclesiastes 1:8; (10) 1 Timothy 6:8; (11) 1 Samuel 2:1; (12) Psalms 5:11; (13) Psalms 23:6; (14) John 15:16.

28

COURAGE

*A Breakthrough Prayer for a Woman Who
Needs Greater Courage in Her Life*

Key Scripture: *"Be strong in the Lord, and in the
power of His might"* (Eph. 6:10).

Prayer: Lord God, I pray now in the name of
my Lord Jesus Christ and I declare that you are
my light and my salvation. Indeed, you are the
strength of my life. Of whom or what, then,
should I be afraid?[1] Through your Spirit, I will
be strong in you, and in the power of your
might.[2] Thank you, Father.

Help me to always be strong in you,
Almighty God,[3] and to remember that there is
never a reason for my heart to fail, because you
will always fight for me.[4] Teach me how to be
of good courage at all times.[5] Show me how I
can mock at fear.[6] Thank you for being the
strength of my life, Father.[7]

Your perfect love casts out all fear in my
life.[8] Thank you for your immeasurable love
which is the most excellent way for me.[9]
Because of you, I will be of good courage, and
I know you will always be there to strengthen
my heart as I put all my hope in you.[10] Thank
you, Father, for removing all fear from me, and
for always being with me.[11]

Your Word tells me that you have not given me a spirit of fear, but of love, and of power, and of a sound mind.[12] In obedience to you, therefore, I will bring all my thoughts into the captivity of Christ and your Word which tells me not to fear[13] and to be not troubled.[14] I will rise up strong in you, Lord God, and in the power of your might, and I will resist the devil, and all his fiery darts of fear, in the mighty name of Jesus Christ my Lord.[15]

With your help, I will never again be afraid. Instead, I will believe all the promises of your glorious Word.[16] You, Lord God, are my Helper, and I will not fear what others shall do unto me.[17] Thank you for giving me courage, Father.

References: (1) Psalms 27:1-2; (2) Ephesians 6:10; (3) 1 Samuel 4:9; (4) Nehemiah 4:20; (5) 1 Chronicles 19:13; (6) Job 39:22; (7) Psalms 27:1; (8) 1 John 4:18; (9) 1 Corinthians 12:31; (10) Psalms 31:24; (11) Psalms 27:14; (12) 2 Timothy 1:7; (13) Luke 12:32; (14) John 14:27; (15) James 4:7; (16) Mark 5:36; (17) Hebrews 13:6.

29

DANGER

*A Breakthrough Prayer for a Woman
Who Faces Danger*

Key Scripture: *"A thousand shall fall at thy side, and ten thousand at thy right hand; but it shall not come nigh thee"* (Ps. 91:7).

Prayer: O Lord God, I thank you for all the promises of your Word which I choose to believe with all my heart. Show me how to trust you with all my heart and to avoid leaning unto my own understanding. In all my ways, Father, I want to acknowledge you, because I know you will direct my paths.[1] Thank you, Lord God.

Though I walk in the midst of trouble, I know you will revive me.[2] Thank you, Father. I know that you, Lord God, whom I serve, are able to deliver me from the burning fiery furnaces of life.[3] I know that you will be with me in times of danger.

Father, I choose to dwell in the secret place you've provided for me, because I know you to be the Most High. Because I know this is true, I will continue to abide under your shadow.[4] You are my refuge and my fortress. You are my God, and I will trust in you.[5]

Thank you for your promise to deliver me from the snare of the fowler and the noisome pestilence.[6] Thank you for covering me with your feathers as I take refuge beneath your wings. Your truth, almighty Father, is my shield and buckler.[7]

Because of these truths, I will not be afraid of the terror by night, nor of the arrow that flies by day.[8] Neither shall I fear the pestilence that walks in darkness, nor the destruction that lays waste at noonday.[9] Though a thousand may fall at my side, and ten thousand at my right hand, I will not fear, because you have promised it will not come near me.[10] Thank you, Father.

You, Lord God, are my refuge and my dwelling place.[11] I know that no evil will befall me, and no plague will come near my dwelling.[12] Thank you for giving your angels charge over me, to keep me in all my ways.[13] Thank you for the angelic protection you promise to me, Father. I know the angels will bear me up in order to keep me from dashing my foot against a stone.[14]

I set my love upon you, dear Father. Thank you for your promises to deliver me and to set me on high, because I know your name.[15] Thank you, also, for all the prayer promises of your Word which show me that

when I call upon you, I will receive your
protection. Thank you for being with me in
trouble, and for delivering and honoring me.[16]

I am at peace, Father, because I know you
are protecting me from all danger. These
things I pray in the incomparable name of your
Son, Jesus Christ.[17] Amen.

References: *(1) Proverbs 3:5-6; (2) Psalms 138:7;*
(3) Daniel 3:17; (4) Psalms 91:1; (5) Psalms 91:2;
(6) Psalms 91:3; (7) Psalms 91:4; (8) Psalms 91:5;
(9) Psalms 91:6; (10) Psalms 91:7; (11) Psalms 91:9;
(12) Psalms 91:10; (13) Psalms 91:11; (14) Psalms
91:12; (15) Psalms 91:14; (16) Psalms 91:15;
(17) John 16:23.

30

DEPRESSION

A Breakthrough Prayer for a Woman
Who Feels Depressed

Key Scripture: *"Out of the depths have I cried unto thee, O Lord"* (Ps. 130:1).

Prayer: Out of the depths have I cried unto you, O Lord God.[1] Let your ears be attentive to my prayer.[2] My soul waits for you, and in your Word I do hope.[3]

I come to you, Father God, in the wonderful name of my Lord Jesus Christ and I confess the depression that I'm experiencing to you. By so doing, I am expressing my earnest desire to forsake it and to put it behind me forever. Thank you for lifting me from the miry clay of depression and setting my feet upon the solid confidence of your Word.[4] Lord God, you are my glory, and the lifter of my head. As I cry unto you I know you are hearing me out of your holy hill.[5]

In my times of depression I sometimes feel as if you have forsaken me, but I know this is not true.[6] I am desperate and needy. Answer me quickly, O God.[7] Restore unto me the joy of your salvation.[8] In your joy I find my strength.[9]

Bring my soul out of prison, that I may praise your name.[10] I call upon your name, Lord God, out of what seems to be a low dungeon to me.[11] You are my hope, O Lord God, and you are my trust.[12] Help me to trust you with all of my heart, not leaning unto my own understanding. As I acknowledge you in all my ways, I know you will direct my paths.[13]

I lift up my eyes unto the hills, realizing that my help comes from you, Father.[14] Thank you for delivering me from all depression. I express faith to you that you will not leave my soul desolate.[15]

Through your grace, I will not fear, because I know you are with me, and I will not be dismayed, because you are my God.[16] Turn my sorrow into joy, Father,[17] as I hold on to the faith you've imparted to me, which is the substance of the things I hope for and the evidence of things I do not see.[18]

Father, thank you for lifting depression from me and delivering me from all the power of darkness and redeeming me through the blood of Jesus.[19]

References: *(1) Psalms 130:1; (2) Psalms 130:2; (3) Psalms 130:5; (4) Psalms 40:2; (5) Psalms 3:3-4; (6) Psalms 22:1; (7) Psalms 70:5; (8) Psalms 51:12; (9) Nehemiah 8:10; (10) Psalms 142:7; (11) Lamentations 3:55; (12) Psalms 71:5; (13) Proverbs 3:5-6; (14) Psalms 121:1; (15) Psalms 141:8; (16) Isaiah 41:10; (17) John 16:20; (18) Hebrews 11:1; (19) Colossians 1:13-14.*

31

DILIGENCE

A Breakthrough Prayer for a Woman
Who Wants to Be More Diligent

Key Scripture: *"Be steadfast, immovable, always abounding in the work of the Lord, knowing that your labor is not in vain in the Lord"* (1 Cor. 15:58, NKJV).

Prayer: Lord God, it is my earnest desire to be diligent in my devotion to you. Help me to be steadfast, immovable, and always abounding in your work, because I know my labor is never in vain in you.[1] Thank you for the promises of your Word, Father.

Help me to serve you with all my heart and all my soul, O Lord.[2] I prepare my heart to serve you alone, O God.[3] With your help, I will never turn aside from following you.[4] I reverence your name as I endeavor to serve you in truth with all my heart.[5]

My heart and soul are set to seek you, Lord God,[6] with a perfect heart and a willing mind.[7] I know that as I seek you, I will find you.[8] My soul thirsts for you.[9] Therefore, I seek you, Lord God, in all your strength, and I will seek your face forevermore.[10]

Help me to sanctify you, Lord God, in my heart of hearts,[11] and to stand fast in you.[12] Be with me, Father, as I study to be quiet, and to mind my own business.[13] Guide me in my study of your Word so that I will meet your approval and become a diligent worker who never needs to be ashamed.[14]

Wonderful God, I believe that all your promises to the diligent are for me. I thank you for the fact that your blessing is always with those who are diligent,[15] and I delight in the understanding of your Word which tells me that diligence is my most precious possession.[16] I will walk in the way of righteousness, Father, because I know that in its pathway there is no death.[17]

I claim your promises that my diligence will lead to prosperity,[18] will nourish my soul,[19] will enable good planning,[20] and will allow me to take my place among the leaders.[21] Thank you for all the promises of your Word which show me that diligence is a key to success in every area of my life. In Jesus name I pray.[22] Amen

References: (1) 1 Corinthians 15:58; (2) Deuteronomy 10:12; (3) 1 Samuel 7:3; (4) 1 Samuel 12:20; (5) 1 Samuel 12:24; (6) 1 Chronicles 22:19; (7) 1 Chronicles 28:9; (8) 2 Chronicles 15:2; (9) Psalms 63:1; (10) Psalms 105:4; (11) 1 Peter 3:15; (12) Philippians 4:1; (13) 1 Thessalonians 4:11; (14) 2 Timothy 2:15; (15) Proverbs 10:4; (16) Proverbs 12:27; (17) Proverbs 12:28; (18) Proverbs 10:4; (19) Proverbs 13:4; (20) Proverbs 21:5; (21) Proverbs 13:4; (22) John 15:16.

32

DIVORCE

A Breakthrough Prayer for a Divorced Woman

Key Scripture: *"I am not alone, because the Father is with me"* (John 16:32).

Prayer: Heavenly Father, as I come to you now in the wonderful name of Jesus Christ, my Lord, I rejoice in the promises of your Word which assure me that I am not alone because you are with me.[1] Thank you for your great love which casts out all fear from my life.[2] I know you will never leave me nor forsake me.[3] Thank you, Father.

I express faith to you, Lord God, that all things will work together for my good even in the aftermath of my divorce, because I love you and I know you have called me according to your purpose.[4] Therefore, I will seek first your kingdom, and your righteousness, realizing, Father, that as I do so, everything in my life will be taken care of.[5] Thank you so much.

Thank you for supplying all my needs according to your riches in glory, through Christ Jesus.[6] Through Him, I can do all things,[7] but without Him, I can do nothing.[8] Christ in me is my hope of glory.[9] Thank you, Father, for allowing your Son to take up residence in my heart.[10]

O Lord God, be near to me.[11] You are my Rock.[12] Thank you for coming to me with your blessed comfort.[13] I take rest in the knowledge that you, Father, are love.[14] Thank you for loving me.

With your help, Father, I refuse all condemnation that the enemy and man would try to put upon me.[15] Deliver me from all unhealthy emotional ties to my ex-husband and all others. Thank you, Father, for accepting me and loving me with your great mercy.[16] Thank you for the liberty you've provided to me in order to enable me to have the freedom to live my life as I should.[17] I praise you, Lord God, for the thoughts you think toward me — thoughts of peace and not of evil. Thank you so much for giving me a future and a hope.[18]

As I call upon you I know you are listening. Through seeking you I've found you, and I will continue to seek you with all my heart.[19] I richly rejoice in your promise that declares that I not only will find you, but you are bringing me back from my captivity.[20] Hallelujah!

References: (1) John 16:32; (2) 1 John 4:18; (3) Hebrews 13:5; (4) Romans 8:28; (5) Matthew 6:33; (6) Philippians 4:19; (7) Philippians 4:13; (8) John 15:5; (9) Colossians 1:27; (10) Galatians 2:20; (11) Psalms 38:21; (12) Psalms 42:9; (13) John 14:18; (14) 1 John 4:8; (15) Romans 8:1; (16) Psalms 86:13; (17) Romans 8:21; (18) Jeremiah 29:11; (19) Jeremiah 29:13; (20) Jeremiah 29:14.

33

DOUBT

*A Breakthrough Prayer for a Woman
Who Struggles With Doubt*

Key Scripture: *"Help thou mine unbelief"*
(Mark 9:24).

Prayer: Father in heaven, there are times when
I struggle with doubt in my life. Help me to
overcome all unbelief in my life, I pray.[1] I want
to be a woman of great faith. Help me to
remember at all times that nothing is too hard
for you, Father.[2]

Help me to trust in you at all times.[3] As I
pour out my heart before you, Father, I realize
that you are my refuge.[4] All my strength is in
you.[5] As I put my unswerving trust in you, I
know I am safe.[6] You are my salvation, Lord
God; I will trust in you, and not be afraid.[7]
Instead of being filled with fear, I will believe
your Word.[8]

Thank you for the wonderful prayer
promise you've given to me, that I will receive
the things I desire when I pray as long as I truly
believe.[9] I want to be a woman of faith, not
doubt, dear Father.

Lord God, I believe that all things work
together for good in my life because I love you,
and I know you have called me according to

your purpose.[10] Help me to remember that whatever is not of faith is sin.[11] Assist me in standing fast in the faith you've imparted to me.[12]

Through your grace, Father, I will walk by faith and not by sight.[13] Help me to hold tightly to the shield of faith with which I will be able to quench all the fiery darts of doubt that come my way.[14]

Help me to hold fast the profession of my faith without wavering,[15] because I realize that without faith it is impossible to please you, Father.[16] I will feed upon your Word daily and receive the faith that comes as I hear your words.[17] I dedicate myself to being strong in faith, giving all the glory to you,[18] Father, and I know that as I do so, all doubt will flee from me.[19] These things I pray and believe in Jesus wonderful name.[20] Amen.

References: *(1) Mark 9:24; (2) Genesis 18:14; (3) Psalms 62:8; (4) Psalms 62:8; (5) Psalms 84:5; (6) Proverbs 29:25; (7) Isaiah 12:2; (8) Matthew 8:26; (9) Mark 11:24; (10) Romans 8:28; (11) Romans 14:23; (12) 1 Corinthians 16:13; (13) 2 Corinthians 5:7; (14) Ephesians 6:16; (15) Hebrews 10:23; (16) Hebrews 11:6; (17) Romans 10:17; (18) Romans 4:20; (19) James 4:7; (20) John 15:16.*

34

ENCOURAGEMENT

*A Breakthrough Prayer for a Woman
Who Needs Encouragement*

Key Scripture: *"Do not fear or be discouraged"*
(Deut. 1:21, NKJV).

Prayer: Lord God, my heavenly Father, I come
to you now in the wonderful name of Jesus my
Lord, and I thank you for the fact that I do not
ever need to fear or be discouraged.[1]
Therefore, I will stand still and await your
salvation which I believe you will reveal to me
this very day.[2] Thank you for fighting for me,
Father, and enabling me to hold my peace.[3]
With your help, I will be strong and I will walk
in good courage.[4]

Thank you for enabling me to live above
fear, Lord God, and keeping me from all
discouragement.[5] Your Word shows me that I
can accomplish what needs to be accomplished
because you are with me.[6] Thank you, O Lord,
my God.

Through you, I will be strong and
courageous. I will not be afraid or dismayed.[7]
Your perfect love, dear Father, has removed all
fear from me, and I trust you to keep me from
ever being faint-hearted again.[8] I believe your
Word, and I desire to walk uprightly according

to its precepts, and I know this is the source of encouragement for me.[9]

You, Lord God, are the strength of my life,[10] and this fact greatly encourages me. You enable me to be of good courage.[11] Thank you for encouraging me and strengthening my heart as I continuously hope in you.[12]

Father, I receive great encouragement from you as I find my total strength in you, and in the power of your might.[13] Thank you for encouraging my heart.

References: *(1) Deuteronomy 1:21; (2) Exodus 14:13; (3) Exodus 14:14; (4) Deuteronomy 31:6; (5) Isaiah 35:4; (6) Jeremiah 1:8; (7) 2 Chronicles 32:7; (8) Isaiah 7:4; (9) Micah 2:7; (10) Psalms 27:1; (11) 1 Chronicles 19:13; (12) Psalms 31:24; (13) Ephesians 6:10.*

35

ENVY

A Breakthrough Prayer for a Woman
Who Struggles With Envy in Her Heart

Key Scripture: *"Where envying and strife is, there is confusion and every evil work"* (James 3:16).

Prayer: My heavenly Father, I repent of the sin of envy which is leading me into strife, confusion, and evil.[1] I want to obey your commandment never to covet or to hold envy and jealousy in my heart.[2] Help me, Lord God, to never envy the status or possessions of others.[3]

Teach me how to be content with what I have, Father, because I realize that godliness with contentment is great gain for me.[4] Give me each day my daily bread.[5]

Teach me not to fret because of the prosperity of evil-doers.[6] The sin of envy makes me angry toward myself and others,[7] and that's why I forsake it now, Father. Through Jesus Christ I can do all things.[8] I never want my heart to envy others again.[9] Instead, I will be kind, tender-hearted,[10] forgiving,[11] and I will honor others[12] at all times.

Father, thank you for showing me that wrath is cruel, anger is outrageous, and envy will keep me from standing.[13] I renounce all envy now as I seek your wisdom[14] and strength.[15] It is my heart-felt desire, Lord God, to walk in love,[16] and I know as I do so, I will be able to put all envy behind me.

Thank you, Father, for forgiving me of the sin of envy,[17] and for delivering me from its evil grip in my life.[18] In Jesus' name I pray.[19] Amen.

References: *(1) James 3:16; (2) Exodus 20:17;*
(3) Deuteronomy 5:21; (4) 1 Timothy 6:6;
(5) Matthew 6:11; (6) Psalms 37:7; (7) Proverbs
6:34; (8) Philippians 4:13; (9) Proverbs 23:17;
(10) Ephesians 4:32; (11) John 20:23; (12) Philippians
2:3; (13) Proverbs 27:4; (14) James 1:5; (15) Nehemiah
8:10; (16) Ephesians 5:2; (17) 1 John 1:9; (18) Matthew
6:13; (19) John 15:16.

36

ETERNAL LIFE

*A Breakthrough Prayer for a Woman
Who Wants to Know She Has Eternal Life*

Key Scripture: *"For God so loved the world, that he gave his only begotten Son, that whosoever believeth in him should not perish, but have everlasting life"* (John 3:16).

Prayer: Dear God, thank you for sending Jesus to die for my sins. I believe in Him, and because I do, I accept your promise of eternal life.[1] I am so grateful for your assurance that I will never perish.[2] To me, Jesus truly is living water.[3]

Father, I have sinned and fallen far short of your glory,[4] but you have commended your love toward me in that, even while I was a sinner, you gave me your love through Jesus Christ.[5] Thank you for your marvelous gift of eternal life.[6]

I believe your Word, Father, and I receive the everlasting life you promise to me.[7] I accept Jesus as being the living bread which came down from heaven, and as I partake of Him, I know I shall live forever.[8] Thank you, Father.

My Savior, Jesus Christ, is the resurrection and the life.[9] He is the way, the truth, and the life for me.[10] Because I live and believe in Him, I know I shall never die.[11] Thank you for all the promises of eternal life contained within your Word, Father.

I thank you so much for everything, Lord God, but especially for the victory I have through my Lord Jesus Christ.[12] Through Him, I lay hold on eternal life, to which I have been called.[13]

You, Father, have given me eternal life in your Son.[14] How I praise you that goodness and mercy shall follow me all the days of my life, and I will dwell in your house forever.[15]

References: (1) John 3:16; (2) John 3:15; (3) John 4:10-14; (4) Romans 3:23; (5) Romans 5:8; (6) Romans 6:23; (7) John 5:24; (8) John 6:51; (9) John 11:25; (10) John 14:6; (11) John 11:26; (12) 1 Corinthians 15:57; (13) 1 Timothy 6:12; (14) 1 John 5:11; (15) Psalms 23:6.*

37

EVANGELISM

A Breakthrough Prayer for a Woman
Who Wishes to Be an Effective Witness for Christ

Key Scripture: *"But you shall receive power when the Holy Spirit has come upon you; and you shall be witnesses to Me in Jerusalem, and in all Judea and Samaria, and to the end of the earth"* (Acts 1:8, NKJV).

Prayer: Lord God, thank you for saving me,[1] for empowering me by your Holy Spirit, and calling me to be a witness for Jesus Christ, my Lord and Savior.[2] I want to be the most effective witness possible, and I ask for your help. Help me to declare your glory everywhere I go, and to tell people of your marvelous works.[3] I want to make your deeds known amongst the people, Father.[4]

It is my heart-felt desire, Lord God, to be a true follower of Jesus, and I ask you to make me a fisher of people through Him.[5] I want to fully obey His command to go forth, teaching all nations.[6] Help me to go into the world, and preach the gospel to others.[7] I want to bear fruit for you, Father.[8]

Open the eyes of the people with whom I share your glorious gospel.[9] Turn them from darkness to light, and from the power of Satan unto you, O God, that they may receive forgiveness of sins, and inheritance among them which are sanctified through faith in the Lord Jesus Christ.[10] In all my ways, Father, I want to acknowledge you.[11] I want to confess Jesus Christ to all I come in contact with.[12]

I will speak the things which I have experienced and received from your Word.[13] Help me to walk in wisdom before others,[14] and to never be ashamed of my Lord's testimony.[15] Thank you for enabling me to be an effective witness, Father.

References: (1) Mark 16:16; (2) Acts 1:8; (3) 1 Chronicles 16:24; (4) Psalms 105:1; (5) Matthew 4:19; (6) Matthew 28:19; (7) Mark 16:15; (8) John 15:16; (9) Acts 26:18; (10) Acts 26:18; (11) Proverbs 3:6; (12) Luke 12:8; (13) Acts 4:20; (14) Colossians 4:5; (15) 2 Timothy 1:8.

38

FAITH

A Breakthrough Prayer for a Woman
Who Wants to Be Filled With Faith

Key Scripture: *"So then faith comes by hearing, and hearing by the word of God"* (Rom. 10:17, NKJV).

Prayer: O Lord God, thank you for all the promises of your Word. I believe that all things truly do work together for good in my life because I love you.[1] I also believe that nothing is too hard for you.[2] You are my lamp, O Lord God.[3] Help me to trust in you at all times,[4] for whom have I in heaven but you?[5] Because I have placed my trust in you, Lord God, I know I will live in safety.[6] Thank you so much.

Your Word teaches me that faith comes from hearing, and that hearing comes from your Word.[7] Help me, Father, to study your Word faithfully, and to walk in its precepts at all times.[8] Increase my faith, Lord God.[9]

Realizing that all things are possible to a person who truly believes, I want to be such a person from now on, Father,[10] and I ask you to enable me to stand fast in the faith you've given to me,[11] because I know that it is by faith that I am able to stand.[12] Through your grace, I want to walk by faith, not by sight.[13] Thank you for enabling me to do so, Father.

Help me to hold fast the profession of my faith without wavering,[14] to pray in faith at all times,[15] to please you through faith as I come before you,[16] to contend for the faith that was once delivered to the saints,[17] to fight the good fight of faith,[18] and to express my faith in you at all times.

As you empower me, Father, I will take the shield of faith you've given to me, and I will use it to quench all the fiery darts of the wicked.[19] Thank you for building my faith, Lord God. In Jesus' name I pray. Amen.

References: *(1) Romans 8:28; (2) Genesis 18:14; (3) 2 Samuel 22:29; (4) Psalms 62:8; (5) Psalms 73:25; (6) Proverbs 29:25; (7) Romans 10:17; (8) 2 Timothy 2:15; (9) Luke 17:5; (10) Mark 9:23; (11) 1 Corinthians 16:13; (12) 2 Corinthians 1:24; (13) 2 Corinthians 5:7; (14) Hebrews 10:23; (15) James 1:6; (16) Hebrews 11:6; (17) Jude 3; (18) 2 Timothy 4:7; (19) Ephesians 6:16.*

39

FEAR

A Breakthrough Prayer for a Woman
Who Wants Freedom From Fear

Key Scripture: *"Let not your heart be troubled, neither let it be afraid"* (John 14:27).

Prayer: Dear Father, thank you for the promises of your Word. With your help, I will not let my heart be troubled or afraid.[1] Help me to remember that I do not have to live in fear any more, because I know you are with me.[2] I believe you will always fight for me, Father,[3] and you will be my protector at all times.[4]

Show me how not to be afraid or dismayed, because I know you go with me wherever I go.[5] Thank you, Father. Through your grace, I will fear no evil, because I know you are with me.[6] You, Lord God, are my light and my salvation. What, then, shall I fear, and of whom shall I be afraid?[7]

Father-God, I have placed my unswerving trust in you. Therefore, I will walk in fear no longer.[8] You are my helper.[9] Thank you for enabling me to dwell in your secret place, Most High God, and for allowing me to abide under your shadow.[10] You are my fortress and my God, and I will trust in you,[11] because I know you will deliver me from the snare of the enemy and from all harmful influences.[12]

You, O God, have not given me a spirit of fear, but of power and of love and of a sound mind.[13] And so now I resist the spirit of fear, in the name of Jesus, and I command it to depart from me. I take my stand on the authority of your Word.[14]

Thank you, Father, for covering me with your feathers. Under your wings I take my refuge. Your truth is my shield and buckler.[15] You, Lord God, are my refuge and my dwelling-place, and because this is true, I know no evil shall befall me.[16] Thank you for giving your angels charge over me, to keep me in all my ways.[17]

Thank you, Father, for your perfect love which has cast out all fear from my life.[18]

References: (1) *John 14:27;* (2) *Genesis 26:24;* (3) *Deuteronomy 3:22;* (4) *Psalms 119:117;* (5) *Joshua 1:9;* (6) *Psalms 23:4;* (7) *Psalms 27:1;* (8) *Psalms 56:4;* (9) *Hebrews 13:6;* (10) *Psalms 91:1;* (11) *Psalms 91:2;* (12) *Psalms 91:3;* (13) *2 Timothy 1:7;* (14) *James 4:7;* (15) *Psalms 91:4;* (16) *Psalms 91:9;* (17) *Psalms 91:11;* (18) *1 John 4:18.*

40

FINANCIAL BREAKTHROUGH

A Breakthrough Prayer for a Woman
Who Is Experiencing Financial Difficulties

Key Scripture: *"Without faith it is impossible to please him* [God]: *for he that cometh to God must believe that he is, and that he is a rewarder of them that diligently seek him"* (Heb. 11:6).

Prayer: Almighty God, my heavenly Father, I worship and adore you. It is with great diligence that I seek you for the breakthrough I need in the realm of my personal finances.[1] I believe all the promises of your Word, which unlock the doors of faith for me to enter into all you have for me. Therefore, I ask for a financial miracle from your hands, and I ask in faith, nothing wavering.[2] I believe you are leading me, guiding me, blessing me, and rewarding me. Thank you, Father.

O God, you are more than able to take care of all my financial difficulties, because you know exactly what needs to be done and what steps need to be taken. I trust in you with all my heart, without leaning toward my own understanding. In all my ways I acknowledge you, Father, and I know you are directing my steps toward financial freedom. Let your resources flow freely from the place of excess to my place of need.[3]

Enable me to manage the financial resources you give to me more effectively so that I will be free to serve you more fully, and to give to the important causes of your kingdom, Father.[4] Responding in obedience to your Word, I ask you to command your blessing upon my finances and upon all that I do.[5]

Deliver me, O my God,[6] from financial pressures, for I know you are my hope.[7] I will hope in you continually, and yet praise you more and more.[8]   I cast all my cares, worries, and anxieties upon you, because I know you care for me.[9] You are my strength in the midst of trouble,[10] and I know you are walking with me in this situation. Therefore, I will keep my mind focused upon you and I will trust in you, knowing that you will keep me in your perfect peace.[11] Thank you, Father, for all you have done and are doing in my life and my finances.

References: (1) Hebrews 11:6; (2) James 1:6; (3) 2 Corinthians 8:14; (4) Proverbs 11:25; (5) Deuteronomy 28:8; (6) Psalms 71:4; (7) Psalms 71:5; (8) Psalms 71:14; (9) 1 Peter 5:7; (10) Psalms 37:39; (11) Isaiah 26:3.

41

FORGIVENESS

*A Breakthrough Prayer for a Woman Who
Wants to Walk in Forgiveness Toward Others*

Key Scripture: *"If ye forgive men their trespasses,
your heavenly Father will also forgive you"* (Matt. 6:14).

Prayer: O heavenly Father, thank you for
showing me the importance of forgiveness.
Help me to practice forgiveness in all the
relationships of my life, and thank you for
promising to forgive me when I do so.[1] You are
so merciful, Lord God, and you do not retain
your anger forever.[2] I want to become more
like you.

I am so happy because you have forgiven
me of all my transgressions,[3] and I want to
forgive others as well.

Through faith, I extend my forgiveness
to any and all who have wronged me, and I
will let all bitterness, wrath, anger, clamor,
and evil speaking be put away from me, along
with all feelings of malice toward others.
With your help, Father, I will be kind to
others, tender-hearted, and forgiving, even as
you have forgiven me in Christ.[4] Thank you
for revealing this to me, Father.

Help me to remember that I should forgive
my offenders at all times, because this brings

relief and release to both me and them.⁵ Father, in Jesus' name, and in obedience to your Word, I specifically forgive the following people:____ _____. By faith, I totally and completely forgive each one who has trespassed against me.⁶ I release them to you, and I pray that you will bless them.⁷ Help me to remember the example of Jesus who said, "Father, forgive them for they know not what they do."⁸

Your Word tells me, Father, that I don't wrestle against flesh and blood, but against unseen forces of evil in the spiritual realm.⁹ Just knowing this, helps me to understand who my true enemy is — the devil — and he comes to steal, plunder, and kill. Father, stop his strategies against my life in every way as I resist the devil,¹⁰ and bring every thought unto the captivity of Christ.¹¹

Even as Christ has forgiven me, I will forgive others.¹² Help me, Father, to walk in love¹³ and forgiveness wherever I go.

References: *(1) Matthew 6:14; (2) Jeremiah 3:12; (3) Psalms 32:1; (4) Ephesians 4:31-32; (5) 1 Peter 2:19-24; (6) Matthew 18:21-22; (7) Matthew 6:14-15; (8) Luke 23:34; (9) Ephesians 6:12; (10) James 4:7; (11) 2 Corinthians 10:5; (12) Colossians 3:13; (13) Ephesians 5:2.*

42

GOD'S LOVE

A Breakthrough Prayer for a Woman
Who Wants to Experience God's Love More Fully

Key Scripture: *"The Lord has appeared of old to me, saying: 'Yes, I have loved you with an everlasting love; therefore with lovingkindness I have drawn you'"* (Jer. 31:3, NKJV).

Prayer: Lord God, thank you for your everlasting love.[1] Truly, your lovingkindness is better than life to me,[2] but there are times when I do not experience your love as fully as I would like. Help me to see that your mercy is great unto heaven,[3] and it always reaches me as well. Give me your wisdom, Father, so that I will be able to understand your lovingkindness more fully.[4]

I draw near to you, Lord God, and I know you are drawing near to me.[5] Thank you, Father, for your great love which dispels all fear from my life.[6] Thank you for commending your love toward me when I was yet a sinner[7] by sending Christ to die for me[8] so that I would never perish but have everlasting life.[9] I receive your love, dear Father.

Thank you for filling my heart with your love by your Holy Spirit.[10] I want always to love you with all my heart, soul, mind, and strength[11] because you have first loved me.[12]

I rejoice in your amazing love, Father.[13] Thank you for loving me, and for showing your love for me by giving Jesus to die for me.[14] Truly I am loved, and nothing shall ever be able to separate me from your love in Christ Jesus, my Lord.[15] Hallelujah! I thank you that your love is poured forth into my heart by the Holy Spirit who you have given to me.[16]

I praise you, Father, for filling me, surrounding me, covering me and enveloping me with your rich and wonderful love which is so abundant that it is truly immeasurable. All these things I pray in the incomparable name of Jesus my Lord.[17] Amen.

References: (1) Jeremiah 31:3; (2) Psalms 63:3; (3) Psalms 57:10; (4) James 1:5 & Psalms 107:43; (5) James 4:8; (6) 1 John 4:18; (7) Romans 5:8; (8) John 3:16; (9) John 3:17; (10) Romans 5:5; (11) Matthew 22:37-38; (12) 1 John 4:19; (13) 1 John 4:16; (14) Ephesians 5:2; (15) Romans 8:35-39; (16) Romans 5:5; (17) John 16:23.

43

GOSSIPING

*A Breakthrough Prayer for a Woman
Who Wants to Stop Gossiping*

Key Scripture: *"A whisperer separateth chief friends"* (Prov. 16:28).

Prayer: O Lord God, I come to you in the name of Jesus, and I ask you to deliver me from gossiping. I never want to be a whisperer who causes problems in my relationships or the relationships of others.[1] Help me to be a person who can keep secrets, not a tale-bearer who reveals secrets.[2] I want to speak your words, O Lord God, not words of gossip or slander.[3] O Lord God, open my lips so that my mouth will show forth your praise.[4]

I happily and willingly choose to forsake all gossiping from this time on and forever. Keep me firmly in your grip, dear Father, so that whenever I am tempted to gossip, your Holy Spirit will immediately convict me so that I can quickly respond in the power of your Spirit[5] with the sword of the Spirit,[6] against any temptation to practice gossip or slander in any form. It is my heart's desire to obey your Word at all times, and you command me never to go about as a talebearer.[7] Teach me your ways in all things,[8] dear Father.

Set a watch, Father, before my mouth. Keep the door of my lips,[9] because I know that sin always exists in the multitude of words.[10] Help me to speak good words in due season.[11] I never want to be rash with my mouth, Father.[12] With your help, I will always say and do everything to your glory, dear God.[13]

Let my speech be always with grace, seasoned with salt, so that I will know what I am to say to others.[14] Give me your wisdom, Father.[15] Through your grace, I will shun vain babblings and all forms of evil gossip.[16] Continue to reveal to me that the tongue can be a fire that sets ablaze a whole world of iniquity.[17]

You have promised me good days, Father, if I will learn to refrain my tongue from evil (including gossip and slander), so I ask you to help me to obey you in this always.[18] I pray that my word will minister grace to those who hear me.[19] Thank you for freeing me from the power of gossiping, Father.

References: (1) Proverbs 16:28; (2) Proverbs 11:13; (3) Numbers 22:38; (4) Psalms 51:15; (5) Ephesians 6:10; (6) Ephesians 6:17; (7) Leviticus 19:16; (8) Psalms 27:11; (9) Psalms 141:3; (10) Proverbs 10:19; (11) Proverbs 15:23; (12) Ecclesiastes 5:2; (13) Colossians 3:17; (14) Colossians 4:6; (15) James 1:5; (16) 2 Timothy 2:16; (17) James 3:6; (18) 1 Peter 3:10; (19) Ephesians 4:29.

44

GRIEF

A Breakthrough Prayer for a Grieving Woman

Key Scripture: *"Behold, and see if there be any sorrow like unto my sorrow"* (Lam. 1:12).

Prayer: Dear heavenly Father, as I come to you now in the name of your Son Jesus, it seems to me as if there is no one who can know the depths of my sorrow except you.[1] Jesus said, "Blessed are those that mourn, for they shall be comforted,"[2] but, Lord God, it seems to me that I'm so far removed from any comfort in my life.

I call upon you to heal my broken heart and to bind up all my wounds.[3] The sorrow within my heart threatens to break my spirit, Father.[4] Somehow, Lord God, miraculously turn my sorrow into joy,[5] as only you can do.

Father, I seek your comforting presence. Help me to believe the promises of your Word. Keep me from fear as I realize you are with me, and express faith to you that you are blessing me with the knowledge that you have overcome the world.[6] You, O Lord God, are my shield. You are my glory, and the lifter of my head.[7] You are making me lie down in green pastures, and you are restoring my soul.[8] Thank you, Father.

Comfort me, Lord God,[9] as these tears flow from my eyes.[10] I come unto you with all my burdens, and as I do so, I experience the rest you've provided for me.[11] Thank you, Father.

Father of mercies, and God of all comfort,[12] fill me with your peace[13] now as I pray.

References: *(1) Lamentations 1:12; (2) Matthew 5:4; (3) Psalms 147:3; (4) Proverbs 15:13; (5) John 16:20; (6) John 16:33; (7) Psalms 3:3; (8) Psalms 23:3; (9) Isaiah 66:13; (10) Lamentations 1:16; (11) Matthew 11:28; (12) 2 Corinthians 1:3; (13) Romans 5:1.*

45

GUIDANCE

*A Breakthrough Prayer for a Woman
in Need of Guidance*

Key Scripture: *"Thou art my lamp, O Lord"* (2 Sam. 22:29).

Prayer: You are my lamp, O Lord God,[1] and your Word is a lamp unto my feet and a light unto my path.[2] Thank you for your Word which gives me all the guidance I need. Show me your ways, O Lord. Teach me your paths.[3] Be my eyes as I seek your will.[4]

Send out your light and your truth, and let them lead me.[5] You are my God forever, and I know you will be my guide even unto death.[6] Thank you, Father. Teach me your ways, O Lord God, so that I will be able to walk in your truth at all times.[7]

Cause me to know the way wherein I should walk.[8] Your commandment is a lamp, and your law is light to me.[9] You are my everlasting light, dear Father.[10] When I sit in darkness, I know you will be my light.[11] Indeed, you, Lord God, are my light and my salvation. Of what then should I be afraid?[12]

Thank you for the guidance of the Holy Spirit in my life.[13] Help me to always be sensitive to His leading and guidance in my life, because I know that all who are led by your Spirit, Father, are your children.[14] Lead me with your peace[15] which I will allow to rule in my heart.[16] Fill me with your Holy Spirit, Father, as I pray.[17]

Your Son, Jesus Christ, is the Light of the world.[18] He is the way, the truth, and the life to me.[19] Mighty Father, what will you have me to do?[20] I will remember Jesus' words, and I will let His words abide within me.[21] As I do so, I will make straight paths for my feet,[22] and I know you will guide me. Thank you for your guidance in my life, heavenly Father.

References: *(1) 2 Samuel 22:29; (2) Psalms 119:105; (3) Psalms 25:4; (4) Numbers 10:31; (5) Psalms 43:3; (6) Psalms 48:14; (7) Psalms 86:11; (8) Psalms 143:8; (9) Proverbs 6:23; (10) Isaiah 60:19; (11) Micah 7:8; (12) Psalms 27:1; (13) Galatians 5:18; (14) Romans 8:14; (15) Isaiah 55:12; (16) Colossians 3:15; (17) Ephesians 5:18; (18) John 8:12; (19) John 14:6; (20) Acts 9:6; (21) John 15:7; (22) Hebrews 12:13.*

46

GUILT

A Breakthrough Prayer for a Woman
Who Wants Freedom From Guilt

Key Scripture: *"There is therefore now no condemnation to those who are in Christ Jesus, who do not walk according to the flesh, but according to the Spirit"* (Rom. 8:1, NKJV).

Prayer: O Lord, my mighty God, I thank you for the realization that I do not have to feel condemned any longer, because I am in Christ Jesus, and I have determined to walk according to His Spirit throughout the rest of my life.[1] Thank you for the law of the Spirit of life in Christ Jesus who has made me free from the law of sin and death.[2]

Father, thank you for the wonderful freedom I enjoy as your child.[3] Help me to stand fast in the liberty through which Christ set me free so that I will never again be entangled by the yoke of guilt or any other bondage.[4] I believe you have forgiven me of all my sins, and you have cleansed me of all unrighteousness.[5] Thank you, Father.

Lord God, you brought me out of the Egypt of my slavery to sin with your mighty hand and your outstretched arm.[6] You freed me from the chains that long had held me back.[7] You caused me to know the truth, and your truth has made me free.[8] Because of your great love for me, I am now truly free,[9] and guilt no longer has power over me.

Now I serve the risen Christ,[10] and His Spirit gives me liberty.[11] How I praise you for redeeming me through the blood of Jesus Christ.[12] His blood cleanses me from all my sin.[13] Thank you for delivering me from guilt, mighty Father.

References: (1) Romans 8:1; (2) Romans 8:2; (3) 1 Corinthians 7:22; (4) Galatians 5:1; (5) 1 John 1:9; (6) Deuteronomy 26:8; (7) Psalms 68:6; (8) John 8:32; (9) John 8:36; (10) 1 Corinthians 7:22; (11) 2 Corinthians 3:17; (12) 1 Corinthians 7:23; (13) 1 John 1:7.

47

HEALING

*A Breakthrough Prayer for a Woman
Who Needs Healing*

Key Scripture: *"Heal me O Lord, and I shall be
healed; save me, and I shall be saved"* (Jer. 17:14).

Prayer: O Lord God, heal me, and I know I will
be healed,[1] because you are the Lord who heals
me,[2] and it is by the stripes of Jesus that I am
able to experience your healing power.[3] Thank
you for showing me, dear Father, that you
want, above all else, for me to walk in health
and prosperity.[4] I believe the great and precious
promises of your Word, dear Father.[5]

Mighty God, I express faith to you that
you can heal me,[6] make me clean,[7] and give me
wholeness.[8] Thank you for the prayer of faith
which will save me from my sickness.[9] Give
me a merry heart which will do me more good
than a medicine.[10]

Your Word assures me that you will
always seek that which was lost, and bring
again that which was driven away. You will
bind up that which is broken, and you will
strengthen the sick.[11] Thank you for your
mighty strength which is at work in my life
even as I pray, Father.[12]

You are my Great Physician.[13] You are my healing Balm of Gilead.[14] I trust in you with all my heart, leaning not unto my own understanding. In this time of sickness, I acknowledge you, and I know you will direct my paths.[15]

I believe your Word, Father God, which tells me that Jesus himself took my infirmities and bore my sicknesses,[16] and that with his stripes I am healed.[17] Like the woman with the issue of blood I believe that the faith you've imparted to me is making me whole[18] as I now receive my healing by faith.[19]

In the name of Jesus Christ, I will rise up and walk in restored health and long life.[20] Thank you, Father, for healing me.

References: (1) Jeremiah 17:14; (2) Exodus 15:26; (3) Isaiah 53:5; (4) 3 John 2; (5) 2 Peter 1:4; (6) Matthew 8:2; (7) Mark 1:40; (8) Matthew 9:21; (9) James 5:15; (10) Proverbs 17:22; (11) Ezekiel 34:16; (12) Psalms 118:14; (13) Mark 5:28; (14) Jeremiah 8:22; (15) Proverbs 3:5-6; (16) Matthew 8:17; (17) Isaiah 53:5; (18) Mark 5:28; (19) Mark 11:24; (20) Acts 3:6.*

48

HEALTH

A Breakthrough Prayer for a Woman
Who Wants to Be Healthy

Key Scripture: *"Because you have made the Lord, who is my refuge, even the Most High, your dwelling place, no evil shall befall you, nor shall any plague come near your dwelling"* (Ps. 91:9-10, NKJV).

Prayer: Heavenly Father, I thank you for good health, and for your promise that no evil will ever befall me and no plague will come near my home.[1] I believe the promises of your sacred Word, and I receive them as personal promises to me. Thank you, Father.

You are my refuge and my fortress. You are my God, and I put all my trust in you.[2] I know you will keep me healthy, Father, as I continue to trust in you with all my heart and acknowledge you in all my ways.[3] Thank you for the fact that you will deliver me from all snares, including the snare of illness.[4] I rejoice in you, Lord God.

It gives me a great sense of joy to know that you want me to walk in health at all times, Father.[5] Because this is true, I do not have to fear disease or sickness any longer.[6] I know you will take care of me, for you have given your angels charge over me,[7] and you have set your love upon me.[8] Thank you, Father.

Thank you for the faith you've imparted to me which makes me whole.[9] You've given me a merry heart which does me far better than any medicine.[10] Thank you, Father, for your joy which is my strength.[11] How happy I am to know you, and to realize that you are never slack concerning your promises.[12] Indeed, I know that all your promises are YES in Christ Jesus.[13]

I receive fullness of health that you've promised to me as I pray, mighty Father, because I know that when I ask anything in the name of Jesus Christ, you will accomplish it in my life.[14]

References: *(1) Psalms 91:9-10; (2) Psalms 91:2; (3) Proverbs 3:5-6; (4) Psalms 91:3; (5) 3 John 2; (6) Psalms 91:5; (7) Psalms 91:11-12; (8) Psalms 91:14; (9) Mark 5:34; (10) Proverbs 17:22; (11) Nehemiah 8:10; (12) 2 Peter 3:9; (13) 2 Corinthians 1:20; (14) John 15:16.*

49

HOLINESS

A Breakthrough Prayer for a Woman
Who Wants to Walk in Holiness

Key Scripture: *"Ye shall be holy: for I the Lord your God am holy"* (Lev. 19:2).

Prayer: O Lord my God, help me to walk in complete holiness before you as I endeavor to be more like you.[1] I realize that no one is as holy as you,[2] but through Jesus Christ I am able to partake of your holiness.[3] Thank you, Father, for the righteousness you've given to me through my Lord and Savior Jesus Christ.[4]

Holy, holy, holy are you, O Lord of hosts. The whole earth is filled with your glory.[5] Help me to have clean hands and a pure heart so that I shall be able to ascend your holy mountain and stand in your holy place.[6] Thank you for sanctifying me unto holiness before I came forth from my mother's womb.[7]

How I praise you for the cleansing power of your Word.[8] Continue to sanctify me, O God, through your Word of truth.[9] Thank you for working in me to both will and to do your good pleasure,[10] which is producing holiness in me.[11] Thank you for the sanctifying blood of Jesus Christ, my Lord,[12] and the Holy Spirit's work of sanctification in my life.[13] I want to experience your holiness into the very roots of my life, because I know if the root is holy, the branches will be also.[14] Father, I want always to bear the fruit of holiness in my life.

Thank you for making me into your holy temple,[15] and for calling me to a life of holiness.[16] Thank you for sanctifying me and making me one with you.[17] Thank you for sending Jesus, who knew no sin, to become sin for me so that I would become your righteousness in and through Him.[18]

References: *(1) Leviticus 19:2; (2) 1 Samuel 2:2; (3) 1 John 2:29; (4) 2 Corinthians 5:21; (5) Isaiah 6:3; (6) Psalms 24:3-4; (7) Jeremiah 1:5; (8) John 15:3; (9) John 17:17; (10) Philippians 2:13; (11) Philippians 2:15-16; (12) Hebrews 13:12; (13) Romans 15:16; (14) Romans 11:16; (15) 1 Corinthians 6:19; (16) 1 Peter 1:16; (17) Hebrews 2:11; (18) 2 Corinthians 5:21.*

50

HOMOSEXUALITY

A Breakthrough Prayer for a Woman
Who Wants Freedom From Homosexuality

Key Scripture: *"Their women did change the natural use into that which is against nature"* (Rom. 1:26).

Prayer: Heavenly Father, thank you for showing me that homosexuality is not your will for me. I want to experience sexual wholeness in a natural way because I believe this is your will for me.[1] Deliver me from all homosexual lusts, I pray.[2] Help me to remember the words of Jesus who said that if I look upon a woman with lust in my heart it is the same as if I had committed adultery with her.[3] Help me to abstain from all carnal lusts that war against my soul.[4]

Father, with your help, I will walk in your Spirit so as not to fulfill the lusts of my flesh.[5] Help me to always be spiritually minded, because I know that to be spiritually minded is life and peace, but to be carnally minded is to experience death.[6]

In Christ, I am free from homosexuality.[7] Thank you, Father. Help me to walk in the freedom He gives to me, and to stand fast in that liberty so that I will never again be entangled with the yoke of bondage that homosexuality has brought to me.[8] Thank you for showing me the truth which has made me free.[9]

Lord God, I confess my sin of homosexuality. I totally repent of it, and I renounce its control in my life. Please forgive me of my sin and cleanse me from all unrighteousness.[10] I receive your forgiveness and cleansing now as I pray. When my flesh lusts against my spirit, I will pray,[11] because I know you are able to do exceedingly abundantly above all that I could ever ask or think, according to your power which works within me.[12] Through your wonderful grace, I will never again sow to my flesh, because I know whenever I sow to my flesh, I reap corruption.[13] I receive your forgiveness and cleansing now with a grateful heart.[14] Thank you for always providing me with a way of escape whenever I am tempted.[15]

I take my stand upon your promises, Father, knowing that I can do all things through Christ who strengthens me.[16] Thank you for the authority I have over all the power of the enemy that enables me to always resist the spirit of homosexuality. With that authority, I command the spirit of homosexuality to depart from me now and forever in the mighty name of Jesus Christ my Lord.[17]

Thank you for setting me free from homosexuality. I will stand fast in the liberty with which Christ has made me free, and I will never again be entangled with that yoke of bondage.[18] All these things I pray, Father, in the name of Jesus Christ my Lord.[19]

References: *(1) Romans 1:26; (2) Psalms 71:2; (3) Matthew 5:28; (4) 1 Peter 2:11; (5) Galatians 5:16; (6) Romans 8:6; (7) John 8:36; (8) Galatians 5:1; (9) John 8:32; (10) 1 John 1:9; (11) Galatians 5:17; (12) Ephesians 3:20; (13) Galatians 6:8; (14) 1 John 1:9; (15) 1 Corinthians 10:13; (16) Philippians 4:13; (17) Acts 3:16; (18) Galatians 5:1; (19) John 16:23.*

51

HOPE

*A Breakthrough Prayer for a Woman
Who Feels Hopeless*

Key Scripture: *"Now may the God of hope fill you
with all joy and peace in believing, that you may
abound in hope by the power of the Holy Spirit"*
(Rom. 15:13, NKJV).

Prayer: O Lord my God, as I come before you
in the name of Jesus, I wait upon you, because
I know that good things always come to those
who wait upon you.[1] You are my hope, O Lord
God.[2] My soul waits for you.[3]

Bring me out of my hopelessness to
newfound hope and faith. O God, in the
multitude of your mercy, hear me. Deliver me
out of the mire, and do not let me sink.[4] Hear me,
O Lord God, for your lovingkindness is so good
to me. Turn to me according to the multitude of
your tender mercies.[5] Perform your good Word
in my life.[6] As I contemplate who you are and
all you have done, I realize that you think
thoughts of peace, and not evil, toward me,
and you are giving me a future and a hope.[7]
Thank you, mighty God.

Let my life be filled with your hope,
joy, peace, and faith so that I will always
continue to abound in hope through the
power of your Holy Spirit.[8] Even now, as I

pray, I am experiencing your hope as the sure and steadfast anchor of my soul.[9] From now on, I will hope continually, and I will praise you more and more,[10] for Christ in me is the hope of glory.[11] Help me, Father, to always be among the company, who through faith and patience, inherit your wonderful promises.[12]

In your Word do I hope.[13] I put my total, unswerving trust in you, Father, and I ask you not to leave my soul destitute.[14] Help me to trust in you with all my heart instead of leaning toward my own understanding. As I acknowledge you in all my ways, I know you will direct my paths.[15] This fact of your Word gives me great hope, faith, and confidence. Thank you for the promises of your Word, Father, for they are my source of both faith and hope.

I will not fear because I know you are with me, and I will not be dismayed because you are my God.[16] You are my hope, mighty Father.[17] I will now be counted among those who through faith and patience inherit your great and mighty promises.[18]

References: (1) Psalms 37:9; (2) Psalms 71:5; (3) Psalms 130:6; (4) Psalms 69:14; (5) Psalms 69:16; (6) Jeremiah 29:10; (7) Jeremiah 29:11; (8) Romans 15:13; (9) Hebrews 6:19; (10) Psalms 71:14; (11) Colossians 1:27; (12) Hebrews 6:12; (13) Psalms 130:5; (14) Psalms 141:8; (15) Proverbs 3:5-6; (16) Isaiah 41:10; (17) Jeremiah 17:17; (18) Hebrews 6:12.

52

HYSTERECTOMY

A Breakthrough Prayer for a Woman
Who Has Had a Hysterectomy.

Key Scripture: *"Let the peace of God rule in your hearts"* (Col. 3:15).

Prayer: Heavenly Father, as I begin this new season in my life, I ask that you would let your peace rule in my heart at all times.[1] I love your truth and peace.[2] Thank you for giving me peace with you through my Lord Jesus Christ.[3]

Because of the peace my Lord Jesus gives to me, I will not be afraid and I will not let my heart be troubled.[4] Thank you for your peace in my life, Father, and for your healing power.[5] You are my glory and the lifter of my head.[6] Though sometimes I feel perplexed, you keep me from despair.[7] Thank you, Father.

To you I will cry, O Lord my Rock. Do not be silent to me. Hear the voice of my supplications when I cry to you, and when I lift up my hands toward your holy sanctuary.[8] Blessed are you, O God, because you have heard the voice of my supplications. You are my strength and my shield. Because my heart trusts in you, I am helped. Therefore, my heart greatly rejoices, and I will praise you with singing.[9]

I will praise you, O Lord God, because you have lifted me up. O Lord my God, I cried out to you, and you healed me. O Lord God, you have brought my soul up from the grave, and you have kept me alive.[10]

I thank you, Father, that you have turned my mourning into dancing for me. You have removed my sackcloth and have girded me with gladness to the end that my glory may sing praises to you, and never again be silent. O Lord my God, I will give thanks to you forever.[11]

References: *(1) Colossians 3:15; (2) Zechariah 8:19; (3) Romans 5:1; (4) John 14:27; (5) Matthew 14:36; (6) Psalms 3:3; (7) 2 Corinthian 4:8; (8) Psalms 28:1; (9) Psalms 28:7; (10) Psalms 30:3; (11) Psalms 30:11-12.*

53

IDENTITY CRISIS

A Breakthrough Prayer for a Woman
Who Is Going Through a Crisis of Personal Identity

Key Scripture: *"Walk worthy of the Lord"* (Col. 1:10).

Prayer: O Lord my God, thank you for enabling me to walk in a way that is worthy of you.[1] Through faith in Jesus Christ, I am able to love others.[2] I desire, my Father, to fully please you, and to be fruitful in every good work as I increase in my knowledge of you.[3] Strengthen me with all might, according to your glorious power so that I will be able to be patient and joyful.[4]

Sometimes I wonder who I really am, Father, but through your Word I know that you have qualified me to be a partaker of the inheritance of the saints in the light.[5] Thank you for delivering me from the power of darkness and conveying me into the kingdom of the Son of your love.[6] In Christ I have redemption through His blood, and all my sins have been forgiven.[7] Thank you, Father.

Because these things are true, I will continue in the faith, grounded and steadfast, and I will not be moved away from the hope of the gospel.[8] I know, dear Father, that it is

Christ in me that is the hope of glory,[9] and I am complete in Him.[10] Thank you, Father. Therefore, as your child, I will put on tender mercies, kindness, humility, meekness, and longsuffering.

With your help, I will bear with others and be forgiving.[11] Through your grace I will put on love, which is the bond of perfection, and I will let your peace rule in my heart, and I will be thankful.[12]

Thank you, Father, for giving me wholeness and helping me to see who I actually am in Christ Jesus and who He is in me.

References: *(1) Colossians 1:10; (2) Colossians 3:14; (3) Colossians 1:10; (4) Colossians 1:11; (5) Colossians 1:12; (6) Colossians 1:13; (7) Colossians 1:14; (8) Colossians 1:23; (9) Colossians 1:27; (10) Colossians 2:10; (11) Colossians 3:13; (12) Colossians 3:14.*

54

IMMORALITY

A Breakthrough Prayer for a Woman
Who Seeks Freedom From Immorality

Key Scripture: *"She that liveth in pleasure is dead while she liveth"* (1 Tim. 5:6).

Prayer: Heavenly Father, I come to you in the mighty name of Jesus Christ my Lord, and I confess my sin of immorality to you with great gratitude for your promise to forgive me of my sins and to cleanse me from all unrighteousness.[1] I no longer want to live in the grip of lustful immorality because I know that's not truly living.[2] Thank you for showing me that carnal mindedness leads to death, but spiritual mindedness is life and peace.[3] Father-God, I want to be spiritually minded from now on.

Remember not the sins of my youth.[4] Because I believe you have freed me from my sins, I covenant with you, Father, to go and sin no more.[5] Thank you for your amazing grace[6] and love.[7] Keep sin from having dominion over me, Lord God, and help me to remember that I am no longer under the Law, but under your wonderful grace.[8]

With your help, I will make no provision for my flesh any longer, because I realize that to do so is to fulfill the lusts of my flesh.[9] Keep me walking in your Spirit, Father, so that I will never again fulfill the lusts of my flesh.[10] Thank you for sending Jesus to die for my sins.[11] Through Him, I now experience full spiritual freedom from immorality.[12] Thank you, Father.

Strengthen me so that I will be able to always stand fast in the liberty with which Christ has set me free, and keep me from ever again being entangled with the yoke of immorality.[13] Thank you, loving God.

References: *(1) 1 John 1:9; (2) 1 Timothy 5:6; (3) Romans 8:6; (4) Psalms 25:7; (5) John 8:11; (6) Ephesians 2:8-9; (7) Romans 5:8; (8) Romans 6:14; (9) Romans 13:14; (10) Galatians 5:16; (11) 1 Corinthians 15:3; (12) John 8:36; (13) Galatians 5:1.*

55

INCEST

A Breakthrough Prayer for a Woman
Who Was the Victim of Incest

Key Scripture: *"There is therefore now no condemnation to those who are in Christ Jesus"* (Rom. 8:1, NKJV).

Prayer: Heavenly Father, thank you for the truth of your Word which assures me that through my Lord Jesus Christ, there is now no condemnation in my life.[1] I believe and I receive that promise now even though the pain and hurt of incest have scarred me in so many ways.

Deliver me from the sense of guilt and shame that has overwhelmed me at times. Let me not be ashamed, and don't let my enemies triumph over me.[2] Deliver me in your righteousness, and cause me to escape from the memories of my past.[3] Bring my soul out of prison, that I may praise your name.[4]

Lord of hosts, you are my Redeemer, and I know you are strong.[5] You deliver and rescue me, and you are working signs and wonders in my life.[6] Heal all my inner hurts, I pray,[7] and release me from all emotional attachments to my abuser.[8] By faith, I choose to forgive him.

Help me, Father God, to walk in forgiveness toward him at all times.[9]

I have sought you, Lord God, and I know you have heard me. Thank you for delivering me from all my fears.[10] Thank you for healing my memories and my hurts.[11] Thank you for saving me from my distresses.[12] You are the Lord my God, and you have brought me out of the house of bondage.[13]

I rejoice in the deliverance and healing you have provided for me, Father.[14] Thank you for enabling me to walk in wholeness from this time forth.[15]

References: (1) Romans 8:1; (2) 2 Kings 17:39; (3) Psalms 71:2; (4) Psalms 142:7; (5) Jeremiah 50:34; (6) Daniel 6:27; (7) Ezekiel 34:16; (8) Luke 4:18; (9) Ephesians 4:31-32; (10) Psalms 34:4; (11) Jeremiah 17:14; (12) Psalms 107:19; (13) Exodus 20:2; (14) Luke 4:18; (15) Mark 2:17.

56

INCONTINENCE

A Breakthrough Prayer for a Woman
Who Suffers From Incontinence

Key Scripture: *"With his stripes we are healed"* (Isa. 53:5).

Prayer: Dear heavenly Father, I believe the clear statement of your Word which tells me that through the stripes of Jesus I am healed.[1] I receive your healing power in my life right now, and I believe you are healing me of incontinence. Thank you, Father.

Heal me, O Lord God, and I shall be healed.[2] My Savior, Jesus Christ, is the Great Physician of my life.[3] I believe all the healing promises of your Word.

Thank you that you always hasten to perform your Word, Father.[4] I know your Word is alive, and it is powerful — so powerful, in fact, that it is sharper than any two-edged sword.[5] Thank you for your Word's clear truth that healing is your children's bread.[6]

You, mighty God, are the Lord who heals me.[7] I believe you are healing me of incontinence now as I pray, because I know that Jesus took away all my infirmities and sicknesses.[8] Thank you, Father. I believe your Word that assures me that whatever things I desire, when I pray, to believe I receive them from you, Father, and I shall have them.[9] I believe that promise now, Lord God, as I pray.

I receive your healing of my incontinence, and I believe you are fully restoring me to health and vitality, because my faith does not rest in the wisdom of men, but in your great power, Almighty God.[10]

Thank you for forgiving me of all my iniquities and healing me of all my diseases.[11]

References: (1) Isaiah 53:5; (2) Jeremiah 17:14; (3) Matthew 9:22; (4) Jeremiah 1:12; (5) Hebrews 4:12; (6) Mark 7:27; (7) Exodus 15:26; (8) Matthew 8:17; (9) Mark 11:24; (10) 1 Corinthians 2:5; (11) Psalms 103:3.

57

INFERIORITY COMPLEX

*A Breakthrough Prayer for a Woman
Who Suffers From an Inferiority Complex*

Key Scripture: *"You are of more value than many sparrows"* (Matt. 10:31, NKJV).

Prayer: O Lord my God, as I come to you now in the name of my Savior Jesus Christ, I ask you to help me to believe your Word which tells me that I am a woman of value — worth far more than sparrows,[1] and even rubies.[2] Thank you for showing me how much you love me.[3] Thank you for setting your love upon me.[4] Your love for me is an everlasting love,[5] and I rejoice in it.

Your lovingkindness is better than life to me, Father.[6] Thank you for bringing me into your banqueting table, and for putting your banner of love over me.[7] As I draw near to you, I sense you are drawing near to me,[8] and this helps me to see myself as a person of value. Thank you, Father.

I am your child, dear Father.[9] I am fearfully and wonderfully made.[10] I have been bought with a price,[11] the precious blood of Jesus Christ my Lord.[12] I have been born again by the Spirit,[13] and I am the apple of your eye.[14] Thank you, Father.

Thank you for showing me that there is no reason for feelings of condemnation or inferiority in my life any longer,[15] because I know I can do all things through Christ who strengthens me.[16] You, O Lord God, are a God who is full of compassion. You are gracious, longsuffering, and plenteous in mercy and truth.[17] I believe that your mercy is everlasting.[18] Thank you, Father.

I ask you to totally deliver me from all feelings of inferiority, Lord God.[19] I know you have sent me to heal the broken-hearted, and to preach deliverance to the captives.[20] Therefore, I will stand fast in the liberty you've imparted to me, and I will never again permit myself to be entangled with the yoke of bondage to inferiority.[21] Thank you for making me free, Father,[22] and for delivering me from the enemy's deception in my life.[23]

References: *(1) Matthew 10:31; (2) Proverbs 31:10; (3) Romans 5:8; (4) Deuteronomy 7:7-8; (5) Jeremiah 31:3; (6) Psalms 63:3; (7) Song of Solomon 2:4; (8) James 4:8; (9) John 1:12; (10) Psalms 139:14; (11) 1 Corinthians 6:20; (12) 1 Peter 1:19; (13) John 3:5; (14) Deuteronomy 32:10; (15) Romans 8:1; (16) Philippians 4:13; (17) Psalms 86:15; (18) Psalms 100:5; (19) Psalms 71:2; (20) Luke 4:18; (21) Galatians 5:1; (22) John 8:32; (23) Luke 21:8.*

58

INSECURITY

*A Breakthrough Prayer for a Woman
Who Feels Insecure*

Key Scripture: *"Whoever trusts in the Lord shall be safe"* (Prov. 29:25, NKJV).

Prayer: Almighty God, I put all my trust in you, and I will not lean unto my own understanding. In all my ways I will acknowledge you, and I know you will direct my paths.[1] Thank you for your Word, Father, which shows me that you will keep me safe as I learn to trust in you.[2]

You, Lord God, are my shield and my exceeding great reward.[3] You are the horn of my salvation, my high tower, and my refuge.[4] You are also my defense.[5] You are my buckler,[6] and I know you will deliver me out of the hand of my enemies.[7]

I thank you, Father, for the secure knowledge that your hand is upon me for good,[8] and goodness and mercy shall follow me all the days of my life, and I will dwell in your house forever.[9] These facts impart great security to me, Father.

Keep me as the apple of your eye, and hide me under the shadow of your wings.[10] You, mighty Father, are my rock and my fortress. You are my Deliverer and my God.

You are my strength, and I will ever trust in you.[11] I find all my security in you.

I proclaim that I have been set free from insecurity because Jesus Christ is the Lord of my life. Therefore, I determine that I will stand fast in the liberty wherewith Christ has set me free, and I will not be entangled anymore in the yoke of the bondage of insecurity.[12] Instead, I will be strong in you, Lord, and in the power of your might.[13]

I will be strong in faith, giving you all the glory, O God, because I am fully persuaded that what you have promised me in your Word, you are willing and able to perform in my life.[14] Praise you, Lord.

References: (1) Proverbs 3:5-6; (2) Proverbs 29:25; (3) Genesis 15:1; (4) 2 Samuel 22:3; (5) Psalms 59:17; (6) 2 Samuel 22:31; (7) 2 Kings 17:39; (8) Ezra 8:22; (9) Psalms 23:6; (10) Psalms 17:8; (11) Psalms 28:7; (12) Galatians 5:1; (13) Ephesians 6:10; (14) Romans 4:20-21.

59

INSOMNIA

*A Breakthrough Prayer for a Woman
Who Suffers From Sleeplessness*

Key Scripture: *"He gives His beloved sleep"*
(Ps. 127:2, NKJV).

Prayer: Help me, heavenly Father, to remember
your Word when I am having trouble sleeping,
because I believe your promise that you do
give your beloved sleep.[1] I thank you for the
certain knowledge that you never slumber nor
sleep.[2] Therefore, I will keep on working
hard, because I know my labors will bring
about a sleep that is sweet.[3] Perform your
Word in my life, Father,[4] and deliver me from
insomnia, I pray.[5]

Thank you for your promises of rest.[6]
You are my Shepherd, and I trust you to lead
me to the still waters, and to make me lie
down restfully in the green pastures.[7] Restore
my soul, O Lord God, I pray.[8] I believe your
Word, and this enables me to enter the rest
you've provided for me.[9] Thank you, Father.

Incline your ear to me, Lord God, and save
me, heal me, and deliver me from insomnia.[10]
Make your mighty power known unto me.[11]
As I cry to you in moments of sleeplessness, I
ask you to deliver me from all distresses.[12] I

cast all my cares upon you, Father, because I know you care for me.[13] Thank you for giving me your rest,[14] and for helping me to sleep soundly. In Jesus' name I pray.[15] Amen.

References: *(1) Psalms 127:2; (2) Psalms 121:4; (3) Ecclesiastes 5:12; (4) 2 Chronicles 10:15; (5) Psalms 71:2; (6) Hebrews 4; (7) Psalms 23:1-3; (8) Psalms 23:3; (9) Hebrews 4:11-12; (10) Psalms 71:2; (11) Psalms 106:8; (12) Psalms 107:19; (13) 1 Peter 5:7; (14) Hebrews 4:1; (15) John 15:16.*

60

INTIMIDATION

*A Breakthrough Prayer for a Woman Who Feels
Intimidated by Others or the Circumstances of Life*

Key Scripture: *"The Lord is my helper, and I will
not fear what man shall do unto me"* (Heb. 13:6).

Prayer: O heavenly Father, thank you for
being my constant helper. Because I know this
is true, I will not fear what other people or
circumstances shall do unto me.[1] You are my
light and my salvation, of what then should I
be afraid? You are the strength of my life;
therefore, I will fear no one.[2] Thank you for
these precious truths, Father.

Even if I should have to walk through the
valley of the shadow of death, I will fear no
evil, because I know you, Lord God, are always
with me.[3] Thank you for always being with
me.[4] Because I know this is true, I will not be
afraid or intimidated by anyone or anything.
Neither will I be dismayed.[5]

I place my full trust in you, Father, and
because this is true, I will not fear what people
can do unto me.[6] I trust your Word, Father,
which tells me, "Be not afraid of him, saith the
Lord: for I am with you to save you."[7] I
believe you are always with me.

Your Word gives me faith to take my stand against all intimidations. I am strong in you, Lord God, and in the power of your might.[8] I will be of good courage, for you strengthen my heart as I hope in you.[9]

I know you love me, Father,[10] and you have not given me a spirit of fear, but of power, and of love, and of a sound mind.[11] I resist all fear and intimidation now, in Jesus' name, and I command all fear and intimidation to depart from me.

I thank you, O God, for always giving me the victory through my Lord Jesus Christ.[12]

References: *(1) Hebrews 13:6; (2) Psalms 27:1; (3) Psalms 23:4; (4) Jeremiah 42:11; (5) Ezekiel 3:9; (6) Psalms 56:4; (7) Jeremiah 42:11; (8) Ephesians 6:10; (9) Psalms 31:24; (10) John 3:16; (11) 2 Timothy 1:7; (12) 1 Corinthians 15:57.*

61

JUDGMENTALISM

A Breakthrough Prayer for a Woman
Who Wants to Be Free of Judgmentalism

Key Scripture: *"Judge not, that you be not judged. For with what judgment you judge, you will be judged; and with the measure you use, it will be measured back to you"* (Matt. 7:1-2, NKJV).

Prayer: Heavenly Father, I come to you now in the name of Jesus Christ my Lord, and I repent of my critical attitude, and my judgmental spirit. I want to be obedient to Jesus who taught that I should not judge others. When I realize that I will be judged with the same judgment I use, I realize how important it is for me to be free from all judgmentalism in my life.[1] Thank you for forgiving me, Father, and for cleansing me from all unrighteousness.[2] Thank you, also, for enabling me to walk in freedom from judgmentalism. With your continued help, I will not judge others. Instead, I will seek to restore others, and as I do so, I will consider myself, lest I should fall into the same temptation.[3]

Enable me, precious Father, to stand fast in the liberty you've given to me so that I will never again be entangled with a yoke of bondage to judgmentalism.[4] Father, help me to walk in love toward all others,[5] and to bear the burdens of others so as to fulfill the Law of Christ.[6]

Above all things, I want to put on love, which is the bond of perfection,[7] because I realize that when I love others, I am abiding in the light.[8] I want to abide in your light and love, heavenly Father. Thank you for first loving me so that I can now love others.[9]

Father, from this time forward I will avoid all judgmentalism by accepting and receiving others as you have accepted and received me in Christ Jesus.[10]

References: (1) Matthew 7:1-2; (2) 1 John 1:9;
(3) Galatians 6:1; (4) Galatians 5:1; (5) Ephesians 5:2;
(6) Galatians 6:2; (7) Colossians 3:14; (8) 1 John 2:10;
(9) 1 John 4:19; (10) Romans 15:7.

62

KNOWING GOD

*A Breakthrough Prayer for a Woman
Who Wants to Know God Better*

Key Scripture: *"Grow in grace, and in the knowledge of our Lord"* (2 Pet. 3:18).

Prayer: O Lord, my God, help me to grow in both grace and knowledge of you.[1] Through Christ, I am able to get to know you better, because you have revealed yourself to me through Him.[2] Thank you, Father.

You are the Lord my God.[3] Help me to quiet my heart and to be still so that I can get to know you better.[4] Multiply your grace and knowledge to me so that I will truly know you, Father.[5] I praise you, Father, for making known the mystery of your will to me, according to your good pleasure.[6] Thank you for giving me your Holy Spirit who guides me into all truth.[7] You, O God, are the Father of glory and I ask you now to give to me the spirit of wisdom and revelation in the knowledge of you, so that the eyes of my understanding will be enlightened, and I will thereby know what is the hope of your calling, and what are the riches of the glory of your inheritance in the saints, and what is the exceeding greatness of your power to me through faith, according to the working of your mighty power.[8]

Fill me with the knowledge of your will in all wisdom and spiritual understanding, Father, so that I will be able to walk worthy of you unto all pleasing, being fruitful in every good work, and increasing in the knowledge of you at all times.[9] Thank you for making it possible for me to know Christ, and the power of His resurrection in my life.[10]

Father, my Lord and God, how excellent is your name in all the earth. You have set your glory above the heavens.[11] I will praise you, O Lord God, with my whole heart, and I will tell of all your marvelous works.[12] Your words are pure words, like silver tried in a furnace of earth, purified seven times.[13] You are my strength,[14] my rock, my fortress, and my Deliverer.[15]

Thank you for being everything to me, mighty Father, and for enabling me to get to know you better. I praise you for who you are. I love you, Father. Let me know you better every day.

References: *(1) 2 Peter 3:18; (2) Matthew 11:27; (3) Exodus 29:46; (4) Psalms 46:10; (5) 2 Peter 1:2; (6) Ephesians 1:9; (7) John 16:13; (8) Ephesians 1:17-19; (9) Colossians 1:9-10; (10) Philippians 3:10; (11) Psalms 8:1; (12) Psalms 9:1; (13) Psalms 12:6; (14) Psalms 18:1; (15) Psalms 18:2.*

63

LEADERSHIP

A Breakthrough Prayer for a Woman
Who Wants To Become an Effective Leader

Key Scripture: *"Show them the way wherein they must walk, and the work that they must do"* (Exod. 18:20).

Prayer: Heavenly Father, help me to be the kind of leader who serves as a good role model to those you've put under my charge so that I will more effectively be able to show them the way wherein they should walk, and the work that they must do.[1] Fill me with your Spirit[2] so that I will be able to demonstrate the fruit of your Spirit at all times in my dealings with others.[3]

May I become an able leader who demonstrates reverential fear toward you, Father, and walks in truth at all times.[4] I want to be the kind of leader you want me to be, one who leads by serving others in the manner of Jesus Christ.[5] Wherever you send me, I will go.[6] Anoint me for the leadership you've called me to do.[7] Give me understanding so that I will be able to judge those I lead properly, and I will be able to discern between good and evil.[8]

Empower me to walk before you, Father, in full integrity of heart and in uprightness at all times.[9] May those I lead be happy in the service they provide.[10] Help me to remember that I am the light of the world.[11] Help me to keep on letting my light shine before those I lead so that they will see your good works and glorify you.[12]

Thank you for equipping me to be a leader under you, dear Father.

References: *(1) Exodus 18:20; (2) Ephesians 5:18; (3) Galatians 5:22-23; (4) Exodus 18:21; (5) John 13:12-14; (6) Joshua 1:16; (7) 1 Samuel 16:12; (8) 1 Kings 3:9; (9) 1 Kings 9:4; (10) 1 Kings 10:8; (11) Matthew 5:14; (12) Matthew 5:16.*

64

LONELINESS

A Breakthrough Prayer for a Woman
Who Wants Full Freedom From Loneliness

Key Scripture: *"I am not alone, because the Father is with me"* (John 16:32).

Prayer: Mighty God, I come to you in the name of Jesus who said, "I am not alone, because the Father is with me."[1] I believe you are with me forever,[2] and I know you will never leave me nor forsake me.[3] Thank you, Father.

Set me free,[4] Father, from all the feelings of loneliness, and let all loneliness in my life be replaced with your fullness,[5] as you strengthen me with all your might.[6] I will believe your Word which tells me that I can have fellowship with you, with Jesus Christ my Lord,[7] and with the Holy Spirit.[8] Lord Jesus, I thank you that I am your friend.[9] I believe that you are both my Lord and my friend.[10]

Thank you, Father, for sending your Holy Spirit, the Comforter, to be with me always.[11] I receive the loving presence of your Spirit now as I pray.[12] I know He is with me, and I know He dwells within me.[13] Holy Spirit, I welcome your presence.

It is so wonderful to know that when others forsake me, you will take care of me, Father.[14]   Lead me into the strengthening bands of Christian fellowship, Father, for I know that whoever does your will is my brother and sister.[15] Thank you for all my brothers and sisters in Christ, Father. As I fellowship with others, I will claim your promise which tells me that where two or three are gathered together in your name, you will be there with us.[16] Guide me by your Spirit[17] to walk in the light, as you are in the light, so that I will have true fellowship with you and with other believers. I thank you, Father, for your promise that as I do so, the blood of Jesus Christ cleanses me from all sin and its effects.[18]

I now have boldness to enter into the most holy place of your glorious and loving presence by the blood of Jesus.[19] I will offer the sacrifice of praise to you continually, O God, the fruit of my lips, giving thanks to your name.[20] I have fullness of joy in your presence.[21]

I love you, Father, and I know that you love me.[22] Because you are with me, loneliness is gone.[23]

References: (1) John 16:32; (2) Matthew 28:20; (3) Hebrews 13:5; (4) John 8:36; (5)Ephesians 3:19; (6) Colossians 1:11; (7) 1 John 1:3; (8) 2 Corinthians 13:14; (9) John 15:15; (10) John 15:15; (11) John 14:16-17; (12) John 20:22; (13) John 14:17; (14) Psalms 27:10; (15) Matthew 12:50; (16) Matthew 18:20; (17) Romans 8:14; (18) 1 John 1:7; (19) Hebrews 10:19; (20) Hebrews 13:15; (21) Psalms 16:11; (22) 1 John 4:19; (23) John 16:32.

65

LOSS

*A Breakthrough Prayer for a Woman
Who Has Experienced a Recent Loss*

Key Scripture: *"The Lord is nigh unto them that
are of a broken heart; and saveth such as be of a
contrite spirit"* (Ps. 34:18).

Prayer: Heavenly Father, thank you for being
near to me during my time of loss. Truly, my
heart is broken, and my spirit is contrite.[1] As I
pour out my heart to you over the loss of

_____,

I realize that you are my only refuge.[2] Thank
you, Father, for your promise to heal the
broken in heart, and to bind up those who are
wounded.[3] I claim this promise, and I now
receive your healing for the sorrow, loss, and
grief I feel.[4] I experience your love and
compassion[5] now as I pray.

Thank you for Jesus who is a man of
sorrows and is well-acquainted with grief.[6] I
believe He has the power to change my sorrow
into joy,[7] and I ask for that to happen in my life.
My heart begins to rejoice, Father, when I
realize that Jesus truly has overcome the world.[8]

Help me to really believe that all things
are working together for good in my life,
because you have called me.[9] I reckon, dear

heavenly Father, that the sorrows of loss I'm experiencing during this present time are not worthy to be compared with the glory you are going to reveal to me.[10] Thank you, Father.

Thank you for the comforting presence of the Holy Spirit in my life.[11] I receive His comfort now as I pray. O God, I am not alone, for you are with me.[12] Nothing shall ever separate me from the love of Christ.[13] Through Him, I am more than a conqueror.[14]

Thank you for giving me the breakthrough I need, and for enabling me to rejoice. I praise you, O God, for you always give me the victory through my Lord Jesus Christ.[15]

References: (1) Psalms 34:18; (2) Psalms 62:8; (3) Psalms 147:3; (4) Jeremiah 17:14; (5) Hebrews 4:15; (6) Isaiah 53:3; (7) John 16:20; (8) John 16:33; (9) Romans 8:28; (10) Romans 8:18; (11) John 14:16-17; (12) Psalms 23:4; (13) Romans 8:38-39; (14) Romans 8:37; (15) 1 Corinthians 15:57.

66

LOVE

A Breakthrough Prayer for a Woman
Who Wants to Be Able to Love Others More Fully

Key Scripture: *"He who loves another has fulfilled the law"* (Rom. 13:8, NKJV).

Prayer: Loving Father, help me to always strive to fulfill your law through love.[1] Show me how to bear the burdens of others and thereby fulfill the Law of Christ.[2] Help me to walk in love at all times.[3]

I realize, Lord God, that I am able to love others only because you, who are love,[4] first loved me.[5] Your banner over me was (and is) love.[6] Empower me to be a being of love, also, and to obey the command of Jesus who said, "A new commandment I give unto you, that ye love one another."[7] Through loving acts that I am able to do other people will know that I am a disciple of Jesus Christ,[8] and I very much want other people to realize this.

Let my love be completely free of hypocrisy, Father.[9] Help me to love others as Jesus has loved me.[10] Help me to remember that knowledge puffs up, but love edifies.[11] Father, with your help, I will let love be the theme of my life. Keep me ever mindful of the truths about love — how it suffers long, is kind, does not envy, does not lift itself up, is not puffed up, bears all things, believes all things, hopes all things, and endures all things.[12] That's the kind of love I want in my life, Father — a love that never fails.[13] Help me to be sure that everything I do is done with love,[14] and show me how I can serve others through love.[15]

Thank you for the rewards of loving. I love you, Father, and I thank you that you love me.[16]

References: *(1) Romans 13:8; (2) Galatians 6:2; (3) Ephesians 5:2; (4) 1 John 4:8; (5) 1 John 4:19; (6) Song of Solomon 2:4; (7) John 13:34; (8) John 13:35; (9) Romans 12:9; (10) John 15:12; (11) 1 Corinthians 8:1; (12) 1 Corinthians 13:4-7; (13) 1 Corinthians 13:8; (14) 1 Corinthians 16:14; (15) Galatians 5:13; (16) John 3:16.*

67

LUST

A Breakthrough Prayer for a Woman
Who Wants Freedom From Lust

Key Scripture: *"Walk in the Spirit, and ye shall not fulfil the lust of the flesh"* (Gal. 5:16).

Prayer: Heavenly Father, I want so much to be freed from the instability that lust brings into my life. Show me how to walk in the Spirit so that I will never again be enticed to give fulfillment to the lusts of my flesh.[1] Teach me how to abstain from fleshly lusts that war against my soul,[2] and forgive me for the lust I've felt and acted upon in the past.[3] Thank you for forgiving me of this sin, and for cleansing me of all unrighteousness.[4]

Thank you for showing me that when I reap to my flesh, I shall of my flesh reap corruption.[5] Father, I don't want to reap the corruption that comes from lust which leads to death.[6] Instead, I choose to be spiritually minded, because I know this leads to life and peace.[7]

Give me the power and strength I need to endure temptation, Father.[8] When the temptation of lustful thoughts comes my way again, help me not to be deceived, but to remember that I am tempted when I am drawn away by my own desires and enticed. Then, when my desires have conceived, they give birth to sin, and sin, when it is full-grown, brings forth death.[9]

Father, I repent of all lust as I draw near to you. Thank you for drawing near to me as well.[10] I fully submit my life to you with the promise that I will resist the devil when he endeavors to seduce me, and I know that my submission to you and my resistance toward him will cause him to flee from me.[11] Thank you for delivering me from lust, precious Father.

References: *(1) Galatians 5:16; (2) 1 Peter 2:11; (3) 1 John 1:9; (4) 1 John 1:9; (5) Galatians 6:8; (6) Romans 8:6; (7) Romans 8:6; (8) James 1:12; (9) James 1:15; (10) James 4:8; (11) James 4:7.*

68

MARRIAGE

*A Breakthrough Prayer for a Woman
Who Wants a Better Marriage*

Key Scripture: *"Let the husband render unto the wife due benevolence: and likewise also the wife unto the husband"* (1 Cor. 7:3).

Prayer: Heavenly Father, I come to you in the wonderful name of Jesus my Lord, thanking you for my husband. Help me to render due benevolence, affection, kindness, and consideration toward him, and help him to render due benevolence, affection, kindness, and consideration toward me.[1] Thank you for making us one flesh.[2] Help us to have better communication with each other as we learn to speak the truth in love,[3] and to walk in love toward each other.[4]

Give us both your wisdom[5], discretion,[6] and understanding.[7] Be merciful to us,[8] and bless our marriage. Abide in us, and in our household, as you work in us in so many important ways. I will not forget, nor turn away from the words of your mouth, Father.[9] I will pay attention to your wisdom and lend my ear to your understanding so that I will preserve discretion and my lips will keep knowledge.[10] Help both me and my husband to keep sound wisdom and discretion in our marriage, because

I know they will be life to our souls and they will provide grace in our marriage.[11]

I want my desire to always be toward my husband, Father,[12] so that he will be able to rejoice and be delighted with me.[13] Let me be a virtuous woman who will always be a crown to my husband.[14] May nothing ever bring division between me and my husband.[15]

Father, help me to submit to my husband as unto Christ[16] as you continue to reveal to me that my husband is my head, even as Christ is the head of His church.[17] I choose to be subject to my husband in everything according to your Word.[18]

I pray, dear Father, that you will so work in my husband's life that he will treat me with honor as the weaker vessel, and as an heir together with him of the grace of life, so that his prayers will never be hindered.[19]

Father, I thank you and I praise you for making my marriage better and better everyday.

References: *(1) 1 Corinthians 7:3; (2) Genesis 2:24; (3) Ephesians 4:15; (4) Ephesians 5:2; (5) James 1:5; (6) Proverbs 5:2 ; (7) Proverbs 5:1; (8) Psalms 25:6; (9) Isaiah 55:11; (10) Proverbs 3:21; (11) Proverbs 3:21; (12) Genesis 3:16; (13) Proverbs 5:18; (14) Proverbs 12:4; (15) Matthew 19:6; (16) Ephesians 5:22; (17) Ephesians 5:23; (18) Ephesians 5:24; (19) 1 Peter 3:7.*

69

MASTECTOMY

*A Breakthrough Prayer for a Woman
Who Has Had a Mastectomy*

Key Scripture: *"A merry heart doeth good like a medicine: but a broken spirit drieth the bones"* (Prov. 17:22).

Prayer: Dear heavenly Father, help me to keep my heart merry,[1] because I know it is your joy that gives me the strength I need to keep from sorrow in my time of loss,[2] to keep on keeping on after my mastectomy. Thank you for your great, everlasting love which keeps me from all fear.[3]

I take my stand upon your Word, dear God, and all your promises which are yes in Christ.[4] Therefore, I will not worry or fear, because I choose to cast all my care upon you, knowing that you always care for me.[5]

Thank you for Jesus, my High Priest, who is always touched with the feelings of my infirmities.[6] I know He is interceding for me before your throne, Father, and this knowledge brings me great comfort in this season of my life.[7]

As I pray, I sense and experience the comfort of your Holy Spirit,[8] the healing power of Jesus Christ,[9] your abiding love,[10] and a wonderful peace that surpasses all understanding.[11]

I know you are with me, Lord God,[12] and I know you will never leave me nor forsake me.[13] This certainty enables me to have the confidence to approach your throne of grace, and as I do so, mighty God, I experience your mercy and receive your grace in my time of need.[14] Thank you, Father.

From this time forward, I will be strong in you, Lord God, and in the power of your might.[15] I will be of good courage, and I know you will strengthen my heart.[16] Because you are the strength of my life, I will fear nothing.[17]

In my heart of hearts, dear God, I know that all things work together for good in my life, because I love you and I know you have called me according to your purpose.[18] In Jesus' name I pray.[19] Amen.

References: *(1) Proverbs 17:22; (2) Nehemiah 8:10; (3) 1 John 4:18; (4) 2 Corinthians 1:20; (5) 1 Peter 5:7; (6) Hebrews 4:15; (7) Hebrews 7:25; (8) John 14:16-17; (9) Luke 4:40; (10) Jeremiah 31:3; (11) Philippians 4:7; (12) Psalms 23:4; (13) Hebrews 13:5; (14) Hebrews 4:16; (15) Ephesians 6:10; (16) Psalms 31:24; (17) Psalms 27:1; (18) Romans 8:28; (19) John 16:23.*

70

MATERIALISM

A Breakthrough Prayer for a Woman
Who Wants to Become Less Materialistic

Key Scripture: *"Lay not up for yourselves treasures upon earth, where moth and rust doth corrupt, and where thieves break through and steal"* (Matt. 6:19).

Prayer: Lord God, help me to keep my priorities straight. I want to seek first your kingdom and your righteousness, and in so doing, I know you will take care of everything else.[1] Keep me from laying up treasures for myself upon earth; instead, I want my treasures to be with you in heaven.[2] Father, keep me mindful of the fact that I cannot serve both you and mammon.[3]

Help me to more fully realize that my life does not consist of the things I have accumulated,[4] but my life is fulfilled by your Word.[5] I want to remain focused, Father, on your eternal truths, working not for that which perishes so easily, but working for that which endures throughout eternity.[6] I thank you for showing me the truth that your kingdom does not consist of material possessions, but of righteousness, peace, and joy in the Holy Ghost.[7] Thank you for the righteousness, peace, and joy you've imparted to me through Him.

Father, I ask you to help me to fully understand that the things which are seen are only temporary, but the unseen things are eternal.[8] Let me set my affection on the unseen things, Lord God, not upon the things of this earth.[9]

Father, I commit to you that I will not love the things of the world, nor the things in the world,[10] because it is my desire to love you with all my heart, soul, mind, and strength.[11] Help me to be content with what I have,[12] because I realize that godliness with contentment is great gain for me.[13]

References: *(1) Matthew 6:33; (2) Matthew 6:19; (3) Luke 16:13; (4) Luke 12:15; (5) Luke 4:4; (6) John 6:27; (7) Romans 14:17; (8) 2 Corinthians 4:18; (9) Colossians 3:2; (10) 1 John 2:15; (11) Deuteronomy 6:5; (12) 1 Timothy 6:8; (13) 1 Timothy 6:6.*

71

MENOPAUSE

A Breakthrough Prayer for a Woman
Who Is Going Through Menopause

Key Scripture: *"Hear my prayer, O Lord, and let my cry come to You. Do not hide Your face from me in the day of my trouble; Incline Your ear to me; in the day that I call, answer me speedily"* (Ps. 102:1-2, NKJV).

Prayer: O Lord my God, thank you for always being there for me. I know you are with me as I embark on the present passage of my life, through menopause. Hear my prayer, and let my cry come unto you. I know you will answer me speedily.[1] Thank you, Father, for all the prayer promises of your glorious Word. I know that you will never forsake the righteous.[2]

Father, I also know that you will never leave me nor forsake me.[3] Give me greater wisdom[4] and understanding[5] as I wait upon you.[6] Give me your peace, which surpasses all understanding[7] as I cast my cares upon you because I know you care for me.[8] Replace the stress in my life with your wonderful peace,[9] dear Lord.

Bless me with good health[10] so that I will be able to serve you more effectively. As I wait upon you, I realize that you are renewing my strength,[11] and you are making me merry which does my heart good like a medicine.[12] Through your Holy Spirit, my body is being quickened,[13] and I am experiencing the resurrection power of Jesus Christ, my Lord.[14]

Help me to remember to rejoice evermore,[15] to pray continually,[16] and to give thanks in everything, for I know this is your will for me.[17] Help me to keep my mind stayed on you,[18] Father-God, as I experience this season of my life, for I know this will give me peace. I know and I thank you that you are with me in every time and every season of my life.

Father, I claim your joy to give me strength[19] as I go through the process of menopause. Thank you for always being there for me. These things I pray in the name of Jesus my Lord.[20]

References: (1) Psalms 102:1-2; (2) Psalms 37:25; (3) Hebrews 13:5; (4) James 1:5; (5) Job 12:12; (6) Psalms 27:14; (7) Philippians 4:7; (8) 1 Peter 5:7; (9) John 14:27; (10) Matthew 8:17; (11) Isaiah 40:31; (12) Proverbs 17:22; (13) Romans 8:11; (14) Philippians 3:10; (15) 1 Thessalonians 5:16; (16) 1 Thessalonians 5:17; (17) 1 Thessalonians 5:18; (18) Isaiah 26:3; (19) Nehemiah 8:10; (20) John 15:16.

72

MENSTRUAL CRAMPS

A Breakthrough Prayer for a Woman
Who Is Experiencing the Pain of Menstrual Cramps

Key Scripture: *"Blessed be the Lord, because He has heard the voice of my supplications! The Lord is my strength and my shield; my heart trusted in Him, and I am helped"* (Ps. 28:6-7, NKJV).

Prayer: Sometimes, mighty Father, it seems as if the pain of menstrual cramps threatens to overwhelm me,[1] but I know this is not your will for me. Therefore, I ask you to heal me and to remove my pain, for you are the Lord that heals me.[2] I believe your Word which tells me that Jesus himself took my infirmities and bore my sicknesses.[3] Therefore, I take my stand upon this healing promise, and I receive your healing now as I pray.[4]

In you, O Lord, I put my trust. I will never be ashamed. You deliver me in your righteousness,[5] and I ask you to set me free from the overwhelming pain of menstrual cramps.[6] You are my rock of refuge, and my fortress of defense to keep me from this pain.[7]

Father, you are my rock and my fortress. Your name, O God, is a high tower.[8] You are my strength.[9] Into your hands I commit my life — both body and spirit — because I know you have redeemed me, O Lord God.[10]

I will be glad, Lord God, and I will rejoice in your mercy, because I know you have considered my trouble and you have known my soul in the midst of my pain and adversity.[11]

Thank you, Father, for lifting this pain from me and enabling me to endure. I praise you for delivering me from all overwhelming pain.[12] Thank you for giving me this wonderful breakthrough, and your truth that sets me free.[13]

References: (1) Psalms 25:16-18; (2) Exodus 15:26; (3) Matthew 8:17; (4) Mark 11:24; (5) Psalms 31:1; (6) Isaiah 53:4; (7) Psalms 31:2; (8) Proverbs 18:10; (9) Psalms 31:4; (10) Psalms 31:5; (11) Psalms 31:7; (12) Isaiah 53:4; (13) John 8:32.

73

MENTAL ILLNESS

A Breakthrough Prayer for a Woman
Who Is Mentally Ill

Key Scripture: *"You will keep him in perfect peace, whose mind is stayed on You, because he trusts in You"* (Isa. 26:3, NKJV).

Prayer: Mighty God, my Father, thank you for the promises of your Word. As I face this mental illness, I trust you to give me peace,[1] and to heal me,[2] because I know you are the Lord God who heals me,[3] and by the stripes of Jesus I am healed.[4] Thank you, Father.

How I thank you for the truth that you wish above all things that I would prosper and be in health.[5] I receive your healing now for my mind, soul, and emotions.[6] You have not given me a spirit of fear, but of love, and of power, and of a sound mind.[7] This truth of your Word makes it clear that mental illness is not your will for me. Your will for me, Father, is mental health. Therefore, I pray that your kingdom come, and your will be done,[8] and I ask you to restore me to complete mental health.[9]

Father, I will always seek your face,[10] and I will walk in your ways.[11] Enable me to remain strong in you, Father, and in the power of your might.[12] I will put on your armor faithfully so that I will be able to stand against all the wiles of the devil.[13]

Thank you for showing me that I do not wrestle against flesh and blood, but against principalities, against powers, against the rulers of the darkness of this age, against spiritual hosts of wickedness in the heavenly places.[14] With your armor, I will be able to withstand in the evil day, and having done all, I will keep on standing.[15]

Through your grace, and through faith in your Word, I will take my stand, having my waist girded with truth and wearing the breastplate of righteousness.[16] I will keep my feet shod with the preparation of your gospel of peace.[17] Help me to use the shield of faith with which I will quench all the fiery darts of the wicked one.[18] Through your assistance, Father, I will put on the helmet of salvation to protect my mind, and I will use the sword of the Spirit, which is your Word.[19] Thank you for the power of your Word to renew my mind, and to free me from all mental illness.[20]

References: (1) Isaiah 26:3; (2) Acts 14:9; (3) Exodus 15:26; (4) Isaiah 53:5; (5) 3 John 2; (6) Mark 11:24; (7) 2 Timothy 1:7; (8) Luke 11:2; (9) Psalms 23:3; (10) Psalms 27:8; (11) Psalms 18:21; (12) Ephesians 6:10; (13) Ephesians 6:11; (14) Ephesians 6:12; (15) Ephesians 6:13; (16) Ephesians 6:14; (17) Ephesians 6:15; (18) Ephesians 6:16; (19) Ephesians 6:17; (20) Ephesians 4:23.

74

MIGRAINES

A Breakthrough Prayer for a Woman
Who Suffers From Migraine Headaches

Key Scripture: *"Heal me, O Lord, and I shall be healed"* (Jer. 17:14).

Prayer: Heal me, O Lord God, and I shall be healed.[1] I believe your Word. It is a lamp unto my feet, and a light unto my path.[2] Thank you for all your promises of healing, Father, which I claim for myself right now. I believe that healing is your children's bread,[3] and that with the stripes of Jesus, I am healed.[4] Thank you for Jesus who took my infirmities and bore my sicknesses.[5]

Heal me, Father, and I shall be healed.[6] My faith reaches out to you now, and I receive your healing touch.[7] Father, I know you are hearing this prayer of faith, and you are delivering me from this headache.[8] I trust you to keep me completely free from migraines.

Keep my heart merry, Father, because I know this will do me better than any medicine will.[9] You are my healing balm.[10] I trust you to always make me whole,[11] because I know that, like the woman with the issue of blood, the prayer of faith has saved me from this sickness.[12] Thank you, Father, for healing me of these migraine headaches. All these things I pray in the wonderful name of Jesus.[13] Amen.

References: *(1) Jeremiah 17:14; (2) Psalms 119:105; (3) Mark 7:27; (4) Isaiah 53:5; (5) Matthew 8:17; (6) James 5:15; (7) Mark 11:24; (8) Psalms 34:4; (9) Proverbs 17:22; (10) Jeremiah 8:22; (11) Matthew 9:22; (12) James 5:15; (13) John 16:23.*

75

MINISTRY

*A Breakthrough Prayer for a Woman
Involved in Ministry*

Key Scripture: *"Serve Him in sincerity and in truth"* (Josh. 24:14).

Prayer: Almighty God, I praise you in the mighty name of Jesus Christ, my Lord. It is my heart's greatest desire to serve you in sincerity and in truth.[1] You have given so much to me, and I want to share what you've given to me with others.[2] Help me to feed your sheep,[3] to be a laborer in your harvest,[4] to feed your church,[5] and to labor together with you[6] wherever I go.

I love you, Father, and I know you love me.[7] Thank you for your great love which casts out all my fear.[8] Enable me to always be steadfast, unmoveable, and always abounding in your work, because I know my labors will never be in vain when they are in you.[9] May I never forget that unless you build the house, those who are doing the work are laboring in vain.[10]

Thank you for making me an ambassador for Christ,[11] and for enabling me to be an effective minister of the New Testament.[12] Lord God, I will never be ashamed of the

Gospel of Jesus Christ, because it is your power unto salvation to all who will believe.[13]

Thank you for so enabling and anointing me to do the ministry you've called me to do.[14] I consecrate and surrender myself totally to your will, Father, and I pray not my will but your will be done in me and in my life.[15]

Fill and empower me now by your Holy Spirit, O God, that I may be an effective minister for Jesus Christ.[16] Let your Holy Spirit truly be like a river pouring out of me, producing the ministry and blessing you desire.[17]

As the Holy Spirit guides and anoints me, I will preach the gospel to the poor, heal the broken-hearted, proclaim liberty to the captives and the recovery of sight to the blind, and set at liberty those who are oppressed.[18] I believe that I can do it because greater are you, O God, within me than he who is in the world.[19] Hallelujah!

References: (1) Joshua 24:14; (2) Matthew 10:8; (3) John 21:16-17; (4) Matthew 9:37; (5) Acts 20:28; (6) 1 Corinthians 3:9; (7) John 3:16; (8) 1 John 4:18; (9) 1 Corinthians 15:58; (10) Psalms 127:1; (11) 2 Corinthians 5:20; (12) 1 Timothy 4:6; (13) Romans 1:16; (14) 1 Corinthians 1:21-29; (15) Mark 14:36; (16) Acts 1:8; (17) John 7:38; (18) Luke 4:18; (19) 1 John 4:4.

76

MISCARRIAGE

A Breakthrough Prayer for a Woman
Who Has Experienced a Miscarriage

Key Scripture: *"The Lord is nigh unto them that are of a broken heart; and saveth such as be of a contrite spirit"* (Ps. 34:18).

Prayer: Lord God, my heavenly Father, as I come to you now in the blessed name of Jesus Christ my Lord, I thank you for being near me in my time of grief and sorrow.[1] My eyes pour out tears unto you,[2] because my sense of loss seems too difficult to bear. Your Word assures me, however, dear Father, that you will comfort me in my time of mourning.[3] Thank you for your comfort which I receive as I pray.

Thank you for removing all fear from me, Lord God, and for always being with me.[4] I receive your supernatural peace[5] and comfort.[6] You are my shield, my glory, and the lifter of my head.[7] You are the God of all comfort, my Father of mercies,[8] and I know you will never leave me nor forsake me.[9] Thank you, mighty Father.

I come to you, Lord God, because I need you so much. I believe you will make me lie down in green pastures, and you will

lead me beside the still waters. Thank you
for your promise to restore my soul from the
effects of this loss, trouble, and heartache.[10]   I
receive your healing touch for my soul and
body now as I pray.[11]   Even though loss,
trouble, and heartache have been my portion,
I continue to take delight in your Word,[12]
mighty Father.

Your tender mercies bring comfort to my
heart.[13]   Your Word brings healing to me.[14]
Heal me, O Lord, and I shall be healed.[15]   You
are the Lord that heals me.[16]   I receive your
healing touch and your wonderful comfort
now as I pray, and I rejoice in your presence,
dear God.

References: (1) Psalms 34:18; (2) Job 16:20;
(3) Matthew 5:4; (4) Genesis 26:24; (5) Romans 5:1;
(6) 2 Corinthians 1:3; (7) Psalms 3:3; (8) 2 Corinthians
1:3; (9) Hebrews 13:5; (10) Psalms 23:1-3; (11) Mark
11:24; (12) Psalms 119:143; (13) Psalms 69:16;
(14) Psalms 107:20; (15) Jeremiah 17:14;
(16) Exodus 15:26.

77

MONEY MANAGEMENT

A Breakthrough Prayer for a Woman
Who Wants to Manage Her Money Better

Key Scripture: *"All things come of Thee"*
(1 Chron. 29:14).

Prayer: O Lord God, I realize that all things
come from your hands,[1] including money,
wealth and riches.[2] Thank you for all you've
given to me. Help me, Father, to become a
better steward of the money I have. You
are the one who gives me power to get
money,[3] and I want to manage the money
you give to me more effectively. All that is
in heaven and on earth is yours, Father,[4] and
I'm just a manager of all you entrust to me.

Help me as I endeavor not to set my
heart on riches,[5] or to trust in money rather
than you.[6] Thank you for showing me that
I cannot serve both you and money,[7] Father.
I desire to love you with all my heart, soul,
mind, and strength.[8] Give me your wisdom
so that I might be able to manage my money
more effectively.[9]

I realize, Lord God, that where my
treasure is, there will my heart be also,[10] and
I want my heart to always be with you.[11]
I will seek first your kingdom and your

righteousness, and I know that you will meet all my needs.[12] Thank you, Father.

References: (1) *1 Chronicles 29:14; (2) 1 Chronicles 29:12; (3) Deuteronomy 8:18; (4) 1 Chronicles 29:11; (5) Psalms 62:10; (6) Proverbs 11:28; (7) Matthew 6:24; (8) Luke 10:27; (9) Proverbs 2:6; (10) Matthew 6:21; (11) Matthew 19:21; (12) Matthew 6:33.*

78

MOTHERHOOD

A Breakthrough Prayer for a Woman
Who Wants to Be a Better Mother

Key Scripture: *"Her children arise up, and call her blessed"* (Prov. 31:28).

Prayer: Heavenly Father, it is my strong desire to be the kind of mother whose children will one day rise up and call me blessed.[1] Help me to train them up in the way that they should go so that when they are older they will not depart from your ways.[2] Give my children the grace to receive your sayings as I teach them so that they will have longevity.[3] So work in their lives, dear Father, that they will attend to your Word and incline their ears to your sayings.[4]

Show them, I pray, the importance of studying your Word so that they will be able to rightly divide your truth, workers who will never know shame because they are approved by you.[5] Give me great compassion for my children,[6] so that I will truly understand them. Help me to raise them up in your nurture and admonition,[7] dear Father. Fill me with your Spirit, Father, so that I will walk in love, patience, and all the fruit of the Spirit in my relationships with my children.[8]

Help me to provide well for my children,[9] and to be a good example to them at all times.[10] How I thank you for my children, Father, because they are such a rich inheritance that you have given to me.[11] I will have no greater joy than that of hearing that my children are walking in the truth.[12]

Bring that to pass, dear Father, and thank you for helping me to be the best mother possible. I pray and thank you, Father, in the wonderful name of Jesus.[13]

References: (1) Proverbs 31:28; (2) Proverbs 22:6; (3) Proverbs 4:10; (4) Proverbs 4:20; (5) 2 Timothy 2:15; (6) Isaiah 49:15; (7) Ephesians 6:4; (8) Galatians 5:22-23; (9) 2 Corinthians 12:14; (10) 1 Timothy 4:12; (11) Psalms 127:3; (12) 3 John 4; (13) John 16:23.

79

NERVOUS BREAKDOWN

A Breakthrough Prayer for a Woman
Who Has Experienced a Nervous Breakdown

Key Scripture: *"For God has not given us a spirit of fear, but of power and of love and of a sound mind"* (2 Tim. 1:7, NKJV).

Prayer: O Father-God, as I come to you now in the blessed name of Jesus, I thank you for bringing me through the recent experiences of my life. I claim your promise that you have not given me a spirit of fear, but of power and of love and of a sound mind.[1] I thank you for renewing my mind through the washing of the water of your Word.[2]

Because of your mercies, mighty Father, I present my body (and my mind) as a living sacrifice to you. I pledge to you that I will no longer be conformed to this world, because I know you are transforming me by the renewing of my mind so that I will be able to prove your good, acceptable, and perfect will.[3]

Father, you tell me in your Word that you wish above all things for me to prosper and to be in health.[4] I ask you to heal me now, and I receive your healing touch as I pray.[5]

Fill me with your Holy Spirit,[6] Father, so that I will be able to produce the fruit of your

Spirit in all that I do.[7] Lead me by your Spirit, Lord God.[8] How I thank you that I did not receive the spirit of bondage again to fear, but I have received your Spirit of adoption which makes me cry out, "Abba, Father."[9] I know, dear God, that the sufferings I've gone through are not worthy to be compared with the glory you are going to reveal in me.[10] I rejoice, Lord God, that you are working in me both to will and to do of your good pleasure.[11]

Because you are for me, almighty Father, I know that nothing can any longer be against me.[12] Thank you for the assurance that nothing shall be able to separate me from your healing love — not death nor life, angels nor principalities, things present nor things to come.[13] In all things I am more than a conqueror through Jesus Christ, my Lord.[14]

Thank you for healing me, dear Father, and for giving me a peace that surpasses all understanding.[15] I will let your peace rule in my heart.[16]

References: *(1) 2 Timothy 1:7; (2) Ephesians 5:26; (3) Romans 12:1-2; (4) 3 John 2; (5) Mark 11:24; (6) Ephesians 5:18; (7) Galatians 5:22-23; (8) Romans 8:14; (9) Romans 8:15; (10) Romans 8:18; (11) Philippians 2:13; (12) Romans 8:31; (13) Romans 8:38-39; (14) Romans 8:37; (15) Philippians 4:7; (16) Colossians 3:15.*

80

OBEDIENCE

A Breakthrough Prayer for a Woman
Who Wants to Walk in Obedience to God

Key Scripture: *"Behold, I set before you today a blessing and a curse: the blessing, if you obey the commandments of the Lord your God which I command you today; and the curse, if you do not obey"* (Deut. 11:26-28, NKJV).

Prayer: Father, I want to be your obedient daughter and handmaiden at all times. Give me the grace to obey your commandments faithfully, I pray.[1] All that you speak to me I will do.[2] Give me the grace, Father, to walk in your statutes and to keep your commandments.[3] Keep me from ever turning aside from them.[4] I want to walk in your ways, mighty Father, and to reverentially fear you.[5]

With your help, I will serve you, O Lord my God, with all my heart, soul, mind, and strength.[6] It thrills me to know that you have made me the head, and not the tail, and that you will keep me above only, and not beneath.[7] Lord God, I love your Word, and I will not let your Word depart from my mouth.[8] I will trust you with all my heart, leaning not unto my own understanding. In all my ways I will acknowledge you, and I know you will direct my paths.[9]

Empower me to walk in all your ways,[10] to keep your commandments,[11] and to obey your voice.[12] I receive the ministry of your Holy Spirit to guide me and direct me into all truth.[13] I will obey Him as He leads me.[14]

I desire to serve you in truth, with all my heart,[15] and to hearken to your Word.[16] Teach me to do your will, dear Father.[17] These things I pray in the name of Jesus, my Lord and Savior.[18] Amen.

References: (1) *Deuteronomy 11:26-28;* (2) *Exodus 19:8;* (3) *Leviticus 26:3-4;* (4) *Deuteronomy 5:32;* (5) *Deuteronomy 8:6;* (6) *Deuteronomy 11:13;* (7) *Deuteronomy 28:13;* (8) *Joshua 1:8;* (9) *Proverbs 3:5-6;* (10) *Joshua 22:5;* (11) *Joshua 22:5;* (12) *1 Samuel 12:14;* (13) *John 16:13;* (14) *Romans 8:14;* (15) *1 Samuel 12:24;* (16) *1 Samuel 15:1;* (17) *Psalms 143:10;* (18) *John 15:16.*

81

PATIENCE

*A Breakthrough Prayer for a Woman
in Need of Patience*

Key Scripture: *"Ye have need of patience, that,
after ye have done the will of God, ye might receive
the promise"* (Heb. 10:36).

Prayer: Almighty God, I have need of patience
so that after I do your will, I will be able to
receive your promise.[1] I want to receive the
blessings of your promises. Help me to
develop a more patient attitude at all times,
and to be an imitator of those, who through
patience, inherit the promises.[2] Teach me how
to wait patiently on you, Father,[3] because I
know that your timing is perfect.[4] I believe
that which you've promised to me will surely
come.[5] I will patiently await the fulfillment of
your promises, Father,[6] for you watch over
your Word to bring it to pass.[7] I rejoice that
your Word will never return unto you void; it
will accomplish the purposes for which you
send it.[8]

Help me never to grow weary in well-doing,
because I know in due season I will surely
reap.[9] Thank you, Father. Show me how to be
patient toward all others.[10] I want to be a
woman who is gentle, apt to teach, and patient.[11]

Thank you for hearing my prayer, Father, and for the ministry of your Holy Spirit who is working in me and enabling me to bear the fruit of patience in my life.[12] Thank you for all the precious promises of your Word, O Father.[13] Your Word gives me the faith and confidence to hold onto the certainty that your promise will surely be fulfilled.[14] Your Word is always true, and your faithfulness is unto all generations.[15]

Strengthen me to never grow weary in well-doing, for I know I will reap in due season if I wait for your perfect will to be accomplished.[16] I will let patience have its perfect work in my life, so that, according to your Word, I will be perfect and complete, lacking nothing.[17] These things I pray, Father, in the wonderful name of Jesus my Lord.[18]

References: (1) Hebrews 10:36; (2) Hebrews 6:12; (3) Psalms 27:14; (4) Psalms 18:30; (5) Hebrews 10:36-37; (6) Acts 1:4; (7) Jeremiah 1:12; (8) Isaiah 55:11; (9) Galatians 6:9; (10) 1 Thessalonians 5:14; (11) 2 Timothy 2:24; (12) Galatians 5:22; (13) 2 Peter 1:4; (14) Habakkuk 2:3; (15) Psalms 119:90; (16) Galatians 6:9; (17) James 1:4; (18) John 15:16.

82

PEACE

*A Breakthrough Prayer for a Woman
Who Wants to Walk in Peace*

Key Scripture: *"Seek peace, and pursue it"* (Ps. 34:14).

Prayer: O Lord God, as I come to you now in the wonderful name of Jesus Christ my Lord, I ask you to help me to walk in peace. Give me your grace to seek and pursue peace at all times.[1] I love your truth and peace.[2] Thank you for the peace Jesus has given to me — a wonderful peace that the world cannot give or take away.[3] Through Jesus Christ, I now have peace with you, Father.[4] Thank you so much.

I know, dear God, that you are not the author of confusion, but of peace,[5] and I receive your wonderful gift of supernatural peace as I pray. Truly, it is a peace that surpasses all understanding.[6] Help me to keep my mind stayed upon you, dear Father, because I know this will enable me to walk in perfect peace as I trust you each step of the way.[7]

In Christ, I have my peace,[8] and I will let your peace rule in my heart at all times.[9] Fill me with your Holy Spirit, Father,[10] so that I will be able to bear the fruit of peace in all the relationships and responsibilities of my life. I receive the ministry of the Holy Spirit to enable me to walk in your peace at all times.[11] Help me to be a peace-maker, because I know the fruit of righteousness is sown in peace of them that make peace.[12] Thank you for the gift of peace, Father.

References: *(1) Psalms 34:14; (2) Zechariah 8:19; (3) John 14:27; (4) Romans 5:1; (5) 1 Corinthians 14:33; (6) Philippians 4:7; (7) Isaiah 26:3; (8) Ephesians 2:14; (9) Colossians 3:15; (10) Ephesians 5:18; (11) Galatians 5:22; (12) James 3:18.*

83

PERFECTIONISM

A Breakthrough Prayer for a Woman
Who Seeks Deliverance From Perfectionism

Key Scripture: *"Without Me you can do nothing"*
(John 15:5, NKJV).

Prayer: Heavenly Father, help me to abide in
Jesus so that I will bear much fruit.[1] Sometimes
I drive myself to distraction with my desire to
be perfect. Thank you for showing me that all
I am, have, and do comes from you.[2]

Deliver me from perfectionism.[3] Through
your grace, I have been made a new creation.
The old nature that drives me to perfectionism
has passed away, and you have made all
things new in my life.[4] I am crucified with
Christ. It is no longer I who live, but Christ
lives in me, and the life which I now live in
the flesh I live by faith in the Son of God,
who loved me and gave himself for me.[5]
In Christ I am complete.[6] Fill me with the
knowledge of your will in all wisdom and
spiritual understanding so that I will walk
worthy of you, Lord God, and be fruitful
in every good work as I increase in my
knowledge of you.[7]

Father, you are my light and my salvation,
and you are the strength of my life.[8] I place

all my trust in you, Lord God, and I know that you will direct my paths.[9]

Thank you for delivering me from the power of darkness and translating me into the kingdom of the Son of your love in whom I have redemption through His blood.[10] How I praise you, mighty Father, that I do not have to make myself perfect, but you are working your perfection,[11] holiness,[12] and righteousness[13] into me. I know that you will perfect that which concerns me,[14] and you will complete the work you've begun in my life.[15]

Your Holy Spirit empowers me to accomplish great things.[16] Having begun in the Spirit, Father, I renounce any attempt to make myself perfect by the flesh.[17] Your strength is made perfect in my weakness. Your grace is sufficient for me.[18]

Thank you for delivering me from perfectionism, dear Father.

References: *(1) John 15:5; (2) Colossians 1:15-20; (3) Joel 2:32; (4) 2 Corinthians 5:17; (5) Galatians 2:20; (6) Colossians 2:10; (7) Colossians 1:9-10; (8) Psalms 27:1; (9) Proverbs 3:5-6; (10) Colossians 1:13; (11) Philippians 2:13; (12) Philippians 3:9; (13) 2 Corinthians 5:21; (14) Psalms 138:8; (15) Philippians 1:6; (16)1 Corinthians 2:4-5; (17) Galatians 3:3; (18) 2 Corinthians 12:9.*

84

PHOBIAS

*A Breakthrough Prayer for a Woman
Who Suffers From Phobias*

Key Scripture: *"Do not be afraid, nor be dismayed,
for the Lord your God is with you wherever you
go"* (Josh. 1:9, NKJV).

Prayer: Lord God, thank you for going with
me everywhere.[1] Help me to remember this
when phobias, irrational fears, and anxieties
threaten to dismay me. You are my light and
my salvation, and because this is true, there is
nothing and no one that I should fear.[2] I will
not be afraid of sudden fear or any other kind
of phobia, because you, Lord God, are my
confidence, and I know you will keep me safe
at all times.[3]

Deliver me from all phobias, Father.[4]
Help me to walk in your peace as I keep my
mind stayed on you and trust you.[5] You have
given great peace to me, and I will not let my
heart be troubled or afraid.[6]

Thank you, Father, that I have not
received the spirit of bondage to fear. Instead,
I have received the Spirit of adoption that
causes me to cry, "Abba, Father." Thank you
for adopting me into your family.[7]

Father, I know you are my Helper;
therefore, I will never fear what people or

circumstances can do to me.[8] It's such a
wonderful realization to know that there is
absolutely no fear in your love. In fact, I rejoice
in the certainty that your perfect love casts out
all fear from my life.[9]

Thank you for delivering me from all
phobias and torments of fear. You have not
given me a spirit of fear, for you have given me
a spirit of power, of love, and of a sound
mind.[10] Fill me with your love now as I receive
it by faith in your promise.[11] Your love is
poured forth into my heart by the Holy Spirit
who you have given to me.[12]

Thank you for giving your angels charge
over me, to keep me in all my ways.[13] I rejoice
in their protection, and in the certainty that you
have delivered me from all my phobias and
fears.[14] You, O God, have delivered me from
all the power of darkness and have translated
me into the kingdom of your dear Son, Jesus
Christ.[15] I have been redeemed from the
power of all phobias through the blood of
Jesus my Lord.[16] Praise the Lord.

References: (1) Joshua 1:9; (2) Psalms 27:1-2;
(3) Proverbs 3:25-26; (4) Psalms 34:4; (5) Isaiah 26:3;
(6) John 14:27; (7) Romans 8:15-16; (8) Hebrews
13:6; (9) 1 John 4:18; (10) 2 Timothy 1:7; (11) Mark
11:24; (12) Romans 5:5; (13) Psalms 91:11; (14) Psalms
34:4; (15) Colossians 1:13; (16) Colossians 1:14.

85

PRAISE

A Breakthrough Prayer of Praise to God

Key Scripture: *"Many, O Lord my God, are thy wonderful works"* (Ps. 40:5).

Prayer: Many, O Lord my God, are your wonderful works.[1] I will bless your name forever and ever.[2] I thank you and I praise you for your so great salvation,[3] the redemption you've provided for me through the blood of Jesus Christ,[4] the fact that you've made me a new creation in Him,[5] the power of your Holy Spirit,[6] your healing power,[7] your everlasting love,[8] and all the other wonderful things you've given to me.[9] Blessed are you, O God.[10] I will praise your name with a song, and I will magnify you with thanksgiving.[11] While I live I will praise you, Father.[12]

I sing unto you, O God, because you have triumphed gloriously. The horse and his rider you have thrown into the sea.[13] I will publish your name, and ascribe greatness unto you at all times.[14] I will give glory unto you, dear Father,[15] because you are so highly exalted, O God, the Rock of my salvation.[16] I give thanks to you, and I praise your mighty name.[17]

I will bless you, Lord God, at all times, and your praise shall continually be in my mouth.[18] My soul shall make its boast in you, and the humble will hear of it and be glad.[19] I will magnify your name, and exalt you, mighty Father.[20] I rejoice in you![21]

Great are you, dear God, and you are greatly to be praised.[22] I shout to you with the voice of triumph,[23] for you are the Lord Most High, and you are so awesome![24] You are a great King over all the earth.[25] Thank you for being my God forever and ever.[26]

Holy, holy, holy, Lord God almighty, who was and is, and is to come![27] You are worthy to receive glory and honor and power, for you created all things, and by your will they exist and were created.[28] Hallelujah!

References: (1) Psalms 40:5; (2) 1 Chronicles 16:36; (3) Hebrews 2:3; (4) Ephesians 1:7; (5) 2 Corinthians 5:17; (6) Acts 1:8; (7) Jeremiah 17:14; (8) Jeremiah 31:3; (9) Ephesians 1:3; (10) Psalms 68:35; (11) Psalms 69:30; (12) Psalms 146:2; (13) Exodus 15:1; (14) Deuteronomy 32:3; (15) Psalms 29:1; (16) Psalms 95:1; (17) Psalms 18:1; (18) Psalms 34:1; (19) Psalms 34:2; (20) Psalms 34:3; (21) Psalms 33:1; (22) Psalms 48:1; (23) Psalms 47:1-2; (24) Psalms 47:2; (25) Psalms 47:2; (26) Psalms 48:14; (27) Revelation 4:8; (28) Revelation 4:11.

86

PRAYER

*A Breakthrough Prayer for a Woman
Who Wants to Pray More Effectively*

Key Scripture: *"Call to Me, and I will answer you"* (Jer. 33:3, NKJV).

Prayer: Heavenly Father, thank you for the power of prayer, and for the assurance that you know all my needs before I express them to you.[1] Thank you, also, for your wonderful willingness to meet all my needs according to your riches in glory, by Christ Jesus.[2] You have blessed me with every spiritual blessing, in the heavenly places in Christ.[3]

As I ask, I know it will be given to me. As I seek, I know I will find. As I knock, I know the door shall be opened.[4] The wonderful promises of your Word fill me with great faith for prayer.[5] Thank you for assuring me that whatever I ask for, if I ask with faith, I shall receive.[6]

Help me to remember always to pray in the name of Jesus, for in so doing I know my prayers will be answered so that you, Father, will be glorified in your Son.[7] As I ask and receive, I experience fullness of joy.[8]

Teach me how to pray without ceasing, Father,[9] to pray everywhere without wrath and doubting,[10] and to always ask in faith, nothing wavering.[11] I know that you hear the prayer of faith,[12] and the effectual, fervent prayer of a righteous person always avails much.[13] I thank you, Lord God, that your eyes are watching over me, and your ears are always open to my prayers.[14] Whatsoever I ask, I shall receive of you because I keep your commandments and do what is pleasing in your sight.[15]

Through your grace, I will abide in Christ and let His words abide in me so that my prayers will be answered.[16] Thank you, Father, for giving me the Holy Spirit to guide me into all truth,[17] and to help me when I pray.[18] Let your Holy Spirit be the Spirit of prayer within me to fulfill your Word so that I may pray more effectively with all prayer and supplication in the Spirit.[19]

I commit myself to the study of your Word,[20] and to be led of your Spirit[21] so that I may pray more effectively.

References: *(1) Matthew 6:8; (2) Philippians 4:19; (3) Ephesians 1:3; (4) Matthew 7:7; (5) Romans 10:17; (6) Matthew 21:22; (7) John 14:13; (8) John 15:11; (9) 1 Thessalonians 5:17; (10) 1 Timothy 2:8; (11) James 1:6; (12) James 5:15; (13) James 5:16; (14) 1 Peter 3:12; (15) 1 John 3:22; (16) John 15:4; (17) John 16:13; (18) Romans 8:26-27; (19) Ephesians 6:18; (20) 2 Timothy 2:15; (21) Romans 8:14.*

87

PREGNANCY

*A Breakthrough Prayer for a Pregnant Woman
Awaiting the Birth of Her Child*

Key Scripture: *"For this child I prayed; and
the Lord hath given me my petition which I asked
of him: Therefore also I have lent him to the
Lord; as long as he liveth he shall be lent to the
Lord"* (1 Sam. 1:27-28).

Prayer: Heavenly Father, thank you for giving
me the honor and privilege of bringing a new
person into this world. I prayed for this child
you are giving to me, and I want you to know
that I dedicate him/her to you.[1] Thank you for
granting my petition, Father.[2] I rest secure in
your care.

It is so reassuring to me to know that you
know my child even while he/she is within my
womb.[3] I ask you, Lord God, to sanctify my
child before he/she is born.[4] I accept the child
you are giving to me as a blessed reward from
you, Father.[5]

May my child always be filled with
wisdom, Lord God. To know that you will
grant this prayer fills my heart with joy.[6] I
believe you are hearing and answering my
prayer for the impartation of wisdom to my

child, and already my heart is joyful.[7] Thank you, Father.

I know that my child is fearfully and wonderfully made by you, Father.[8] Cover my womb with your love.[9] I pray that the birthing process will go smoothly,[10] be safe[11] and free of all complications and fear.[12] Thank you for giving me your peace which surpasses all understanding. It surrounds me now, and I know it will also be with me during labor and delivery.

As you bring forth my child from the womb, O God, I pray that you will make him/her to trust you.[13] May he/she be cast upon you from the womb, dear Father, and know you as his/her God.[14] In Jesus' holy name I pray.[15] Amen.

References: *(1) 1Samuel 1:27-28; (2) 1 Samuel 1:27; (3) Jeremiah 1:5; (4) Jeremiah 1:5; (5) Psalms 127:3; (6) Proverbs 15:20; (7) Proverbs 23:24; (8) Psalms 139:14; (9) Psalms 139:13; (10) 1 Timothy 2:15; (11) Psalms 4:8; (12) 1 John 4:18; (13) Psalms 22:9; (14) Psalms 22:10; (15) John 16:23.*

88

PREJUDICE

A Breakthrough Prayer for a Woman Who
Wants Freedom From Being Prejudiced

Key Scripture: *"There is neither Jew nor Greek, there is neither bond nor free, there is neither male nor female: for ye are all one in Christ Jesus"* (Gal. 3:28).

Prayer: Heavenly Father, thank you for showing me that all people, of all races and all backgrounds, are all one in Christ Jesus.[1] Set me free of all prejudice in my life. I realize that prejudice is not pleasing to you. I now know that there is neither Greek nor Jew, circumcision nor uncircumcision, bond nor free, but Christ is all, and He is in all.[2]

I believe that all people are the work of your hands, dear Father,[3] and Jesus died for everyone.[4] Thank you for loving the world so much that you gave your only Son to die for us[5] so that whosoever will may come.[6] I confess my prejudice to you, and I ask you to forgive me and to cleanse me from all unrighteousness.[7] Help me to see others as you see them, and to love them with your love.[8]

Keep me from pre-judging people according to economic standards as well, dear Father, because I know that the rich and the poor meet together, because you are the Maker of them all.[9] Another commonality that I share with all other people is that all are of the dust, and all shall turn to dust again.[10] Thank you for revealing that truth to me, Father.

When I realize that we shall all stand before the judgment seat of Christ,[11] I know that I have no right to pre-judge anyone. Help me to execute true judgment only, and to always show mercy and compassion to others.[12]

When I consider what it is that you require of me, dear Father, I realize that there is no room for prejudice in my life whatever. Therefore, I ask you to help me to do justly, to love mercy, and to walk humbly with you.[13]

References: (1) Galatians 3:28; (2) Colossians 3:11; (3) Job 34:19; (4) Romans 6:10; (5) John 3:16; (6) Acts 2:21; (7) 1 John 1:9; (8) John 15:12; (9) Proverbs 22:2; (10) Ecclesiastes 3:20; (11) Romans 14:10; (12) Zechariah 7:9; (13) Micah 6:8.

89

PREMENSTRUAL SYNDROME

*A Breakthrough Prayer for a Woman Who
Suffers From PMS*

Key Scripture: *"Casting all your care upon Him;
for He careth for you"* (1 Pet. 5:7).

Prayer: Sometimes, dear Father, the PMS
symptoms rob me of my joy, my love, and my
peace. Because I know this is not your will for
me, I gladly cast all my cares upon you now,
because I know you truly care for me,[1] and this
helps me so much. Like the Psalmist, I look
within and say, "Why are you cast down, O my
soul? And why are you disquieted within me?
Hope in God: for I shall yet praise him, who is
the health of my countenance, and my God."[2]
Father, I want to experience your rest,[3] I want
to hope in you,[4] and I want to praise you.[5]

Thank you for letting me know that your
presence goes with me, and you will give me
your rest.[6] You, O God, are my refuge, and I
know your everlasting arms are beneath me.[7]
Thank you, Father.

Throughout this day I will endeavor to
keep my mind focused on you, Father, and I
will trust you, because I know this will give me
your perfect peace.[8] Thank you, Father. My
soul blesses you, Lord God, and I will not forget

all your benefits to me, because I know you forgive me of all my iniquities, and you heal me of all my diseases.[9] Dear Father, I ask you to heal me of PMS and to deliver me from all its effects.

When I am afraid, I will trust in you.[10] Thank you for giving power to me when I feel faint, and for increasing my strength. I wait upon you, Lord God, and as I do so my strength is being renewed and I mount up with wings like an eagle. You enable me to keep on running without being weary.[11] Thank you, Father.

I will believe your Word which tells me that Jesus himself took my infirmities and bore my sicknesses,[12] and that by His stripes I was healed.[13]

Therefore, through faith in you, Father,[14] and your Word, I believe that I receive your healing power now as I pray,[15] for you are my Lord who heals me of PMS.[16] These things I pray and I believe in the wonderful name of Jesus Christ my Savior.[17] Amen.

References: *(1) 1 Peter 5:7; (2) Psalms 43:5; (3) Hebrews 4; (4) Psalms 71:5; (5) Psalms 33:1-4; (6) Exodus 33:14; (7) Deuteronomy 33:27; (8) Isaiah 26:3; (9) Psalms 103:2-3; (10) Psalms 56:3; (11) Isaiah 40:29,31; (12) Matthew 8:17; (13) 1 Peter 2:24; (14) Mark 11:22; (15) Mark 11:24; (16) Exodus 15:26; (17) John 16:23.*

90

PRIDE

*A Breakthrough Prayer for a Woman Who
Wants Freedom From Pride*

Key Scripture: *"Pride goes before destruction,
and a haughty spirit before a fall"* (Prov. 16:18,
NKJV).

Prayer: O Lord my God, I come to you in
the name of Jesus, and I ask you to deliver me
from pride,[1] because I know pride holds
me back from spiritual progress like a
chain around my neck.[2] My pride brings
me great shame.[3] Forgive me of my pride,
and cleanse me from all unrighteousness.[4]
Thank you for showing me that pride goes
before destruction, and a haughty spirit before
a fall.[5] Set me free from the power of pride.[6]

I give all the glory to you, dear Father,
because I understand and I know that you
are the God of the universe.[7] I want to
simply obey your command to not be proud.[8]
Thank you for your Word which warns me
that the proud will be abased. Therefore, I
humble myself under your almighty hand,
knowing that you will exalt me in due time.[9]
Thank you, Father.

Father, you resist the proud, and you
give grace to the humble.[10] I will walk in

humility from this time forth. I know your grace is sufficient for me to do this, Father, and your strength will be made perfect in my weakness.[11] Thank you for sending Jesus who came to give me abundant life.[12] I realize that my pride has prevented me from enjoying the fullness of that abundance, and I renounce it now, fully claiming your promise of abundant life. Thank you, Father.

References: (1) Psalms 71:2; (2) Psalms 73:6; (3) Proverbs 11:2; (4) 1 John 1:9; (5) Proverbs 16:18; (6) John 8:36; (7) Jeremiah 9:24; (8) Jeremiah 13:15; (9) 1 Peter 5:6; (10) 1 Peter 5:5; (11) 2 Corinthians 12:9; (12) John 10:10.

91

PROCRASTINATION

*A Breakthrough Prayer for a Woman Who
Wants Freedom From Procrastination*

Key Scripture: *"Seek the Lord while He may
be found, call upon Him while He is near"*
(Isa. 55:6, NKJV).

Prayer: Heavenly Father, I come to you in the
name of Jesus Christ my Lord, and I confess
that I put off too many things in my life,
including seeking you,[1] prayer,[2] witnessing,[3]
and other responsibilities. Please forgive me
for the sin of procrastination, and cleanse me
from all the unrighteousness it has brought into
my life.[4] Your Word is true in saying that
mischief will come to those who procrastinate.[5]

I want to seize every opportunity you give
to me, Father. I want to be diligent, steadfast,
unmoveable, and always abounding in your
work, Lord God.[6] I want to take advantage of
every present moment of my life.

With your help, O God, I will lay aside
every weight, and the sin of procrastination
which so easily ensnares me, and I will run
with endurance the race that you have set
before me, looking unto Jesus who is the
author and finisher of my faith.[7] Through your
grace, I strengthen my hands and my knees in

order to make straight paths for my feet in order to do your work, Father God.[8]

You are the God of peace and I thank you for bringing up my Lord Jesus from the dead. He is the great Shepherd, and it is His blood of the everlasting covenant that will make me complete in every good work to do His will.

Thank you for your workmanship in my life which enables me to do that which is well pleasing in your sight including walking free of all procrastination. I give you all the glory, Lord.[9]

References: *(1) Isaiah 55:6; (2) 1 Thessalonians 5:17; (3) Acts 1:8; (4) 1 John 1:9; (5) 2 Kings 7:9; (6) 1 Corinthians 15:58; (7) Hebrews 12:1-2; (8) Hebrews 12:12-13; (9) Hebrews 13:20-21.*

92

PROMISCUITY

*A Breakthrough Prayer for a Woman Who
Wants Freedom From Promiscuity*

Key Scripture: *"Flee fornication"* (1 Cor. 6:18).

Prayer: Heavenly Father, as I pray now in the name of Jesus Christ my Savior, I confess the sin of promiscuity. I ask you to forgive me of this sin that I've allowed to come into my life and to cleanse me from all unrighteousness.[1] I commit to flee from fornication,[2] and put it behind me forever. I know that living for sinful pleasure brings spiritual death to me even while I live.[3] Therefore, I seek to become spiritually minded, because I know this will give me life and peace, whereas to be carnally minded leads to death.[4] Thank you for sending Jesus Christ to give me abundant life,[5] and to set me free from the power of promiscuity.[6] I praise you that the law of the Spirit of life in Christ Jesus has set me free from the law of sin and death.[7] I am a new creation in Christ Jesus. The old things are passed away, and all things have become new.[8] I am a new person, and sin cannot rule over me.[9]

Dear God, you gave me this body not for fornication, but to serve you.[10] Because of your great mercies in my life, I present my body to you now, a living sacrifice, holy, and acceptable to you, because I know this is my reasonable service to you, Father. Help me to avoid being conformed to this world, but to be transformed by the renewing of my mind so that I will be able to prove what is your good, acceptable, and perfect will in my life.[11]

Fill me with your Holy Spirit[12] so that I will be able to produce the fruit of your Spirit in all the relationships and responsibilities of my life.[13] I will walk in the Spirit in order to avoid fulfilling the lusts of my flesh.[14] With your help, dear Father, I will abstain from all fleshly lusts, fornication, and promiscuity, because I know these things war against my soul.[15] In the name of Jesus, I bow before you, O God, and I declare by faith that Jesus Christ is Lord over every area of my life including my sexual desires and appetites.[16] I will stand fast in the liberty wherewith Christ has made me free, and I will not be entangled again in the yoke of bondage.[17] Hallelujah! Thank you for freeing me of promiscuity, dear heavenly Father.

References: (1) 1 John 1:9; (2) 1 Corinthians 6:18; (3) 1 Timothy 5:6; (4) Romans 8:6; (5) John 10:10; (6) Romans 6:22; (7) Romans 8:2; (8) 2 Corinthians 5:17; (9) Romans 6:14; (10) 1 Corinthians 6:13; (11) Romans 12:1-2; (12) Ephesians 5:18; (13) Galatians 5:22-23; (14) Galatians 5:16; (15) 1 Peter 2:11; (16) Philippians 2:11; (17) Galatians 5:1.

93

PROMISES OF GOD

A Breakthrough Prayer for a Woman Who
Wants to Claim All of God's Promises

Key Scripture: *"The Lord is not slack concerning His promise"* (2 Pet. 3:9).

Prayer: O Lord my God, I thank you that you are never slack concerning your promises,[1] and I desire to claim, receive, and live by your promises throughout my life. Your wonderful prayer promises fill my heart with faith and joy. I believe your Word which tells me that Jesus said, "Whatsoever you shall ask the Father in my name, he will give it you."[2] Father, I claim that promise now as I pray in the wonderful name of Jesus.

I also claim the promise of your presence. Father, thank you for your presence which goes with me, and provides me with rest.[3] Eternal God, you are my refuge, and underneath me are your strong and everlasting arms.[4] I claim your promise of perfect peace as I focus on you and trust in you.[5] By trusting in you with all my heart, I know that you will direct my paths.[6] Thank you for your willingness to supply all my needs according to your riches in glory through Jesus Christ.[7]

Father, I thank you and praise you that you are able to do exceeding abundantly beyond all that I could ask or think, according to your power that is at work within me.[8] Thank you for forgiving all my iniquities and healing all my diseases.[9] You give power to me when I am faint.[10] You restore my soul.[11] Your goodness and mercy will accompany me throughout my life, and I will dwell in your house forever.[12] Thank you, Father.

With you, mighty Father, all things are possible.[13] All your promises are yes in Christ Jesus.[14] Lord God, I take my stand upon your great and precious promises. I am filled with gratitude that your divine power has given me all things that pertain to life and godliness, and now I know that I'm able to partake of your divine nature, having escaped the corruption that is in the world through lust.[15] Thank you for your promises, Father.

References: *(1) 2 Peter 3:9; (2) John 16:23; (3) Exodus 33:14; (4) Deuteronomy 33:27; (5) Isaiah 26:3; (6) Proverbs 3:5-6; (7) Philippians 4:19; (8) Ephesians 3:20; (9) Psalms 103:2-3; (10) Isaiah 40:29; (11) Psalms 23:3; (12) Psalms 23:6; (13) Matthew 19:26; (14) 2 Corinthians 1:20; (15) 2 Peter 1:3-4.*

94

PROTECTION

*A Breakthough Prayer for a Woman Who
Seeks God's Protection*

Key Scripture: *"God is our refuge and strength, a
very present help in trouble"* (Ps. 46:1).

Prayer: Heavenly Father, thank you for being
my refuge, my strength, and a very present
help in trouble.[1] I seek your protection over
me and my loved ones, and in the shadow of
your wings I will make my refuge.[2] You,
Father, are my Rock of refuge,[3] so continue to
lead me to the Rock that is higher than I.[4]

As you hold me up, I know I will be safe.[5]
Preserve my soul from all evil, Almighty God,[6]
and deliver me from every evil work. Preserve
me unto your heavenly kingdom.[7] Thank you,
Father. You are my Helper, and I will not fear
what man can do unto me.[8]

Thank you for showing me, Lord God,
that nothing shall be able to separate me from
your love, which I've found in Christ Jesus my
Lord — not death, life, angels, principalities,
powers, things present, things to come, height,
depth, nor any other creature.[9]

Thank you, Father. You are my shield, and
the horn of my salvation. You are my high
tower, and my refuge.[10]

In you I place my complete and unswerving trust.[11] I take great comfort in knowing that your eyes are continually upon me, Father,[12] and you are faithfully establishing me and keeping me from all evil.[13]

You are so good, precious Father, and you are my stronghold in the day of trouble.[14] No evil shall befall me, and no plague shall come near my dwelling. You give your angels charge over me to keep me in all my ways.[15] Thank you for providing me and my loved ones with your protection at all times.

References: (1) Psalms 46:1; (2) Psalms 57:1; (3) Psalms 94:22; (4) Psalms 61:2; (5) Psalms 119:117; (6) Psalms 121:7; (7) 2 Timothy 4:18; (8) Hebrews 13:6; (9) Romans 8:38-39; (10) Psalms 144:2; (11) Psalms 11:1; (12) Psalms 33:18; (13) 2 Thessalonians 3:3; (14) Nahum 1:7; (15) Psalms 91:10-11.

95

PURITY

A Breakthrough Prayer for a Woman Who
Seeks Greater Purity in Her Life

Key Scripture: *"Blessed are the pure in heart: for they shall see God"* (Matt. 5:8).

Prayer: O Lord my God, I ask you to enable me to experience full heart-purity so that I will be able to see you clearly.[1] As I ascend your hill, desiring to stand in your holy place, I realize that I need clean hands and a pure heart.[2] You make that possible for me, Father, through Jesus Christ, because His blood cleanses me from all sin.[3]

Thank you for the cleansing and purifying power of your Word.[4] I wash in its clear waters as I meditate upon its truths.[5] My body is your temple, holy Father, and I want my body to be pure and clean before you.[6] Forgive me of all my sins, and cleanse me from all unrighteousness.[7]

It is my desire to keep myself pure at all times, Father,[8] and to cleanse my hands and purify my heart.[9] As I draw near to you, I know you are drawing near to me.[10] Give me the grace to walk in purity, Father, as I submit myself to you and resist the devil.[11] As I

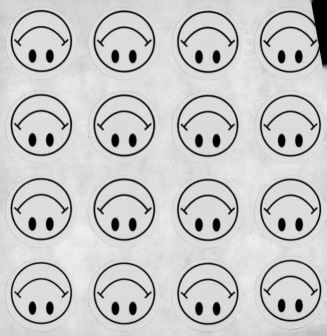

humble myself in your presence, I realize that you are lifting me up.[12] Thank you, Father.

I vow, Father, to cease from all evil.[13] I will keep myself pure.[14] I rejoice, Father, that I have been bought with a price[15] — the precious blood of Jesus my Lord[16] — and I am not my own.[17]

I am a new creation in Christ Jesus,[18] and I pledge to glorify you, O God, in both my body and my spirit which belong to you.[19] I am a temple of your Holy Spirit who teaches me and guides me in the ways of purity.[20]

Thank you, Father, for the joy of walking in purity.

References: (1) Matthew 5:8; (2) Psalms 24:3-4; (3) 1 John 1:7; (4) Ephesians 5:26; (5) Joshua 1:8; (6) 1 Corinthians 3:17; (7) 1 John 1:9; (8) 1 Timothy 5:22; (9) James 4:8; (10) James 4:8; (11) James 4:7; (12) James 4:10; (13) Isaiah 1:16-17; (14) 1 Timothy 5:22; (15) 1 Corinthians 6:20; (16) 1 John 1:7; (17) 1 Corinthians 6:19; (18) 2 Corinthians 5:17; (19) 1 Corinthians 6:20; (20) 1 Corinthians 6:19.

96

RAPE

*A Breakthrough Prayer for a Woman Who
Has Been the Victim of Rape*

Key Scripture: *"God is our refuge and strength, a
very present help in trouble"* (Ps. 46:1, NKJV).

Prayer: Heavenly Father, the pain and anguish
I've acquired as a result of the rape leave me
feeling so overwhelmed, frightened, guilty,
angry, shameful, violated, and depressed. As I
come to you now in the precious name of Jesus
my Lord, I thank you for loving me with your
everlasting love.[1] Your thoughts are upon me,[2]
Lord; you are both my help and my deliverer.[3]

I believe the truth of your Word and it
makes me free.[4] I know that whom the Son
makes free is free indeed, Father, and I want
to walk in the complete freedom,[5] liberty,[6]
and wholeness[7] that you have provided for
me in Christ Jesus.

I want to be free from all fear, Father, and
I ask you to fill me now with your perfect love
that casts out all fear. I believe that you are
lifting every bit of fear from me now.[8] You
have not given me a spirit of fear, Father-God,
but you have given me a spirit of power, and of
love, and of a sound mind.[9] You, O Lord God,
are a shield about me. You are my glory, and

the lifter of my head.[10] Though trouble and anguish took hold of me, your words give me a sense of delight.[11] Thank you, Father.

I ask you to deliver me, O God, from all oppression,[12] confusion,[13] and fear[14] that the enemy tries to put on me. I submit myself to you now, Father, and as I resist the devil he flees from me.[15] I will always overcome him by the blood of the Lamb and the word of my testimony.[16] My enemy does not triumph over me[17] for you, O God, always give me the victory through my Lord Jesus Christ.[18]

I need your healing touch, Lord God. You are the Lord that heals me.[19] Heal me and I shall be healed.[20] I receive your healing touch now as I pray, Father.[21] Heal my feelings, my thoughts, my emotions, and my body.

Thank you for the comforting presence of your Holy Spirit.[22] I lay aside all anxiety about these things as I pray, Father, and I believe that your peace that passes all understanding will guard my heart and my mind through Christ Jesus.[23]

Your face, Lord God, will I always seek.[24] My heart is fixed, O God, my heart is fixed, and I will sing and give you praise.[25] I now cast all my cares upon you, Lord, because I know that you will take good care of me.[26] Teach me your way, Father-God, and lead me in a smooth path.[27] Therefore, I will wait on you and be of good courage. As I do so, precious Father, I realize you are strengthening my heart, healing me, and making me whole.[28]

References: *(1) Jeremiah 31:3; (2) Jeremiah 29:11; (3) Psalm 40:17; (4) John 8:32; (5) John 8:36; (6) Galatians 5:1; (7) Mark 10:52; (8) 1 John 4:18; (9) 2 Timothy 1:7; (10) Psalms 3:3; (11) Psalms 119:143; (12) Psalms 119:134; (13) 1 Corinthians 14:33; (14) 1 John 4:18; (15) James 4:7; (16) Revelation 12:11; (17) Psalms 41:11; (18) 1 Corinthians 15:57; (19) Exodus 15:26; (20) Jeremiah 17:14; (21) Mark 11:24; (22) John 14:16-17; (23) Philippians 4:6-7; (24) Psalms 27:8; (25) Psalms 57:7; (26) 1 Peter 5:7; (27) Psalms 27:11; (28) Psalms 27:14.*

97

REPENTANCE

A Woman's Breakthrough Prayer of Repentance

Key Scripture: *"Return unto Me, and I will return unto you, saith the Lord of hosts"* (Mal. 3:7).

Prayer: Heavenly Father, I come to you now in the name of Jesus Christ my Lord, and I return to you in full repentance of my sins. Thank you for your promise to return to me.[1] As I draw near to you, I thank you that you are drawing near to me.[2] Father, I repent of the following specific sins: _____

_____.

Thank you for forgiving me and cleansing me from all unrighteousness.[3]

As I turn again to you, Lord God,[4] I promise that I will turn from my evil ways, and I will keep your commandments and statutes.[5] Thank you for being my gracious and merciful God, and for your promise not to turn away from me when I return to you.[6] Help me to bring forth fruits that are worthy of repentance.[7]

Father, I rejoice in your goodness which leads me to repentance.[8] I submit myself to you.[9] I humble myself in your presence.[10] I will trust you, Lord God, with all my heart, and I will not lean unto my own understanding. In all my ways, I will acknowledge you, and I know you will direct my paths.[11] Thank you for the gift of repentance, dear Father.

References: (1) *Malachi 3:7;* (2) *James 4:8;* (3) *1 John 1:9;* (4) *2 Chronicles 30:9;* (5) *2 Kings 17:13;* (6) *2 Chronicles 30:9;* (7) *Luke 3:8;* (8) *Romans 2:4;* (9) *James 4:7;* (10) *James 4:10;* (11) *Proverbs 3:5-6.*

98

REST

*A Breakthrough Prayer for a Woman Who
Wants to Experience Rest*

Key Scripture: *"In returning and rest you shall
be saved; in quietness and confidence shall be your
strength"* (Isa. 30:15, NKJV).

Prayer: Heavenly Father, I want more of your
quietness, strength, and confidence,[1] which
comes from the wonderful rest you give to
me.[2] Your Word is a lamp unto my feet, and a
light unto my path.[3] It imparts faith to my
heart, and as I believe your Word, I enter into
your rest.[4] As I am still in your presence, I fully
understand that you are God.[5] Thank you,
Father, for the rest and peace that come through
quietness in your presence. In your presence
there is rest and fullness of joy.[6]

Thank you for keeping me in perfect
peace as I focus on you and trust fully in you.[7]
I rejoice in the peace you've imparted to me,
which the world can neither give nor receive.[8]
Lord God, you are my Shepherd, and because
this is true, I know I will want for nothing.[9]
Thank you for making me to lie down in
green pastures, and leading me beside the
still waters.[10]

Father, as I pray, I realize you are restoring my soul, and leading me in the paths of righteousness for your name's sake.[11] Thank you so much for the restoration and leading you give to me. As your child, I claim your promise that enables me to be led by your Spirit.[12]

I desire to dwell with you all the days of my life, Father, and to behold your beauty as I worship you.[13] I thank you that you will hide me in the day of trouble in your pavilion. In the secret place of your tabernacle you will hide me, and you will set me upon a rock.[14]

Help me to be like Mary who chose the better part of sitting quietly in your presence and learning of you.[15] Thank you, Father, for the strength, peace, rest, and confidence I've received from you as I enjoy the quietness of your presence. I cast all my cares upon you, Father, because I know you care for me, and this gives me great rest.[16]

References: *(1) Isaiah 30:15; (2) Hebrews 4; (3) Psalms 119:105; (4) Matthew 11:28; (5) Psalms 46:10; (6) Psalms 16:11; (7) Isaiah 26:3; (8) John 14:27; (9) Psalms 23:1; (10) Psalms 23:2; (11) Psalms 23:3; (12) Romans 8:14; (13) Psalms 27:4; (14) Psalms 27:5; (15) Luke 10:42; (16) 1 Peter 5:7.*

99

SALVATION

*A Breakthrough Prayer for a Woman
Who Recognizes Her Need for a Savior*

Key Scripture: *"For God so loved the world, that He gave His only begotten Son, that whosoever believeth in Him should not perish, but have everlasting life"* (John 3:16).

Prayer: Heavenly Father, thank you for sending Jesus Christ, your only begotten Son, to be my Savior. I believe in Him, and because I do, I now know that I have everlasting life.[1] Thank you, wonderful Father. As I call upon your name, Lord God, I know you are saving me.[2] I repent of my sins, fully aware that I have sinned and have fallen far short of your glory, Father.[3]

Thank you for commending your love to me, in that while I was yet a sinner, Christ died for me.[4] Even though I now understand that the wages of sin are death, I also realize that your gift to me is eternal life through Jesus Christ my Lord.[5] Thank you, Father, for such an amazingly wonderful gift.

Through your grace, mighty Father, I am saved. I'm so glad you showed me that it's not through works of righteousness which I have done that I am saved, but it's through your grace alone.[6] Dear God, you are my Savior.[7] Thank you for sending Jesus Christ into the world to save sinners.[8]

Through your grace, I am able to confess with my mouth that Jesus is my Lord, and I believe in my heart that you have raised Him from the dead. Through this means, I know that I have been saved.[9] Thank you, Father.

I rejoice in you, O Lord God, because you are the God of my salvation.[10] You are mighty in my midst, and you have saved me, and are rejoicing over me with joy.[11] You have made me a new creature in Christ, the old things are passed away and all things have become new.[12] I have been born again through the incorruptible seed of your mighty Word which lives and abides forever.[13]

Thank you, O God, my Savior, for saving me and setting me free.

References: *(1) John 3:16; (2) Acts 2:21; (3) Romans 3:23; (4) Romans 5:8; (5) Romans 6:23; (6) Ephesians 2:8-9; (7) 1 Timothy 2:3; (8) 1 Timothy 1:15; (9) Romans 10:9; (10) Psalms 24:5; (11) Zephaniah 3:17; (12) 2 Corinthians 5:17; (13) 1 Peter 1:23.*

100

SATANIC ATTACK

A Breakthrough Prayer for a Woman
Who Is Undergoing a Satanic Attack

Key Scripture: *"No weapon that is formed against thee shall prosper; and every tongue that shall rise against thee in judgment thou shalt condemn. This is the heritage of the servants of the Lord, and their righteousness is of me, saith the Lord"* (Isa. 54:17).

Prayer: Heavenly Father, I thank you for the promises of your Word. I claim your promises during this time of satanic attack. I specifically acknowledge your promise that the gates of hell shall not prevail against your people, the Church.[1] I thank you for the equipment and weapons you have given to me to fight against the enemy. I thank you for your armor, and for the sword of the Spirit which is your mighty Word.[2]

Lord, you said in your Word that you have given me authority over all the power of the enemy and nothing shall by any means hurt me.[3] You also said if I submit myself to you and resist the devil, he will flee from me.[4] I resist him now in the power and authority of your Holy Spirit,[5] your Word,[6] and the blood of Jesus Christ.[7]

I resist you, Satan, in the name of Jesus Christ, my Lord and Savior, and I command you to stop interfering in my life. You have no right to me whatsoever, for I am a daughter of God.[8]

Thank you, Lord God, that you do not have to save us with sword and spear.[9] The weapons of my warfare are not carnal, but they are mighty to the tearing down of every satanic stronghold.[10] Help me to remember at all times who you are, Lord, and that you are fighting for me.[11] All power in heaven and on earth are yours,[12] and you are delivering me from the influence and oppression of the enemy.[13] Help me always to remember that the battle really is yours, Father, not mine. As I take my stand upon your Word, in the name of Jesus Christ, by the power of your Holy Spirit, I believe that Satan is fleeing from me.[14] Thank you, almighty God.

As I call upon you, I know you are delivering me, and this leads me to glorify you.[15] Thank you for delivering me according to your Word.[16]

Lord God, you are my defense.[17] You are my Rock of refuge.[18] I find shelter in the blessed promises and provisions of your Word. Therefore, I shall wage a good warfare, as I hold onto my faith, and a good conscience.[19]

Thank you, Father, that no enemy can defeat me.[20] I praise you that nothing shall ever be able to separate me from your love.[21] Hallelujah!

References: (1) Matthew 16:18; (2) Ephesians 6:13, 17; (3) Luke 10:19; (4) James 4:7; (5) Ephesians 6:10-11; (6) Hebrews 4:12; (7) Colossians 1:14; (8) John 1:12; (9) 1 Samuel 17:47; (10) 2 Corinthians 10:4; (11) Psalms 40:13; (12) Matthew 28:18; (13) Psalms 43:1-3; (14) James 4:7; (15) Psalms 50:15; (16) Psalms 119:170; (17) Psalms 7:10; (18) Psalms 94:22; (19) 1 Timothy 1:18-19; (20) 1 John 4:4; (21) Romans 8:39.

101

SELF-CONFIDENCE

*A Breakthrough Prayer for a Woman
Who Needs Greater Self-Confidence*

Key Scripture: *"God hath not given us the spirit
of fear; but of power, and of love, and of a sound
mind"* (2 Tim. 1:7).

Prayer: Heavenly Father, I thank you and
praise you for the wonderful realization that
you have given me a spirit of power and
love and a sound mind in place of a spirit
of fear.[1] This gives me a greater sense of
self-confidence, and I thank you for all you've
done for me and for all you mean to me.
Therefore, I come boldly to your throne of
grace, and as I do so I know I am obtaining
your mercy and finding grace to help me in
my time of need.[2]

I ask you for boldness, Lord, so that
with great power and boldness, I may give
witness to the Resurrection of Jesus Christ.[3] I
am not ashamed of the gospel, because I
know it is your power unto salvation for
all who believe.[4] Thank you, Father.

I know, mighty God, that you are on
my side; therefore, I will not fear.[5] I have no
reason for shame, because I know you and I
believe in you.[6] This enables me to be of

good courage, because you are strengthening my heart as I continue to hope in you.[7] In you, O Lord God, do I place all of my trust,[8] and I realize that this is the key to greater confidence in my life. Thank you, Father.

With you, Almighty Father, nothing is impossible,[9] and all of my self-confidence stems from this blessed truth. Because you are for me, I realize that nothing can be against me.[10] In fact, I can do all things through Christ who strengthens me.[11] Greater is He that is in me than he that is in the world.[12]

Never again will I cast away my confidence in you, Father, because I know it has great reward.[13] I know, because your Word proclaims it, that all things are possible to me when I believe your Word.[14] Thank you, Father.

Lord God, thank you for being my constant helper. Because this is true, I no longer need to fear what others may do to me,[15] and my sense of self-confidence is fully restored. Thank you, Father.

References: *(1) 2 Timothy 1:7; (2) Hebrews 4:16; (3) Acts 4:33; (4) Romans 1:16; (5) Psalms 118:6; (6) 2 Timothy 1:12; (7) Psalms 31:24; (8) Psalms 71:1; (9) Mark 10:27; (10) Romans 8:31; (11) Philippians 4:13; (12) 1 John 4:4; (13) Hebrews 10:35; (14) Mark 9:23; (15) Hebrews 13:6.*

102

SELF-CONTROL

A Breakthrough Prayer for a Woman
Who Needs Greater Self-Control

Key Scripture: *"But the fruit of the Spirit is love, joy, peace, longsuffering, kindness, goodness, faithfulness, gentleness, self-control. Against such there is no law"* (Gal. 5:22-23, NKJV).

Prayer: O mighty God, thank you for filling me with your Holy Spirit,[1] and for enabling me to bear the fruit of your Spirit in all the relationships and responsibilities of my life. I especially thank you for the fruit of self-control,[2] and I pray that you will make me more fruitful with regard to self-control in every area of my life. Because I belong to Christ, I desire to have my flesh, with all its passions and desires, crucified with Him.[3] As I live in the Spirit, I ask for your strength to enable me to walk in the Spirit.[4] I realize, mighty God, that as I walk in the Spirit, I shall not fulfill the lust of the flesh.[5] Thank you, Father.

Therefore, I take good heed toward myself[6] so that I will produce the fruit of self-control wherever I go. Set a watch, O Lord God, before my mouth, and keep the door of my lips.[7] Enable me to rule over my spirit[8] as I endeavor to be sober and vigilant, because I know that my enemy, the devil, wanders about like a roaring lion, seeking whom he may devour.[9] Rebuke him, Father, in the name of Jesus Christ.[10]

O God, help me to control my temper,[11] and to successfully overcome all temptation.[12] Thank you for your great faithfulness in my life, and for your promise to not permit me to be tempted above what I am able to bear, and for your promise to make a way of escape for me.[13]

I rejoice in you almighty God my Father.[14]

References: *(1) Ephesians 5:18; (2) Galatians 5:23; (3) Galatians 5:24; (4) Galatians 5:25; (5) Galatians 5:16; (6) Deuteronomy 4:15; (7) Psalms 141:3; (8) Proverbs 25:28; (9) 1 Peter 5:8; (10) Jude 9; (11) James 1:19; (12) Matthew 26:41; (13) 1 Corinthians 10:13; (14) 1 Thessalonians 5:16.*

103

SHAME

A Breakthrough Prayer for a Woman
Who Lives in Shame

Key Scripture: *"Let me not be ashamed, let not mine enemies triumph over me"* (Ps. 25:2).

Prayer: Lord God, I ask that you help me with the issue of shame that threatens to overwhelm me. Let me not be ashamed, and don't let my enemies triumph over me.[1] Please forgive me my sins, and cleanse me from all unrighteousness.[2] I believe that the blood of Jesus Christ cleanses me from all shame and guilt.[3] Break the power of the stronghold of shame in my life, and bring all of my thoughts and feelings under the Lordship of Jesus Christ.[4]

Thank you for showing me that there is no condemnation to me any more because I am in Christ Jesus. Help me to not walk according to my flesh any longer, but to walk according to the Spirit.[5] Thank you for showing me that the law of the Spirit of life in Christ Jesus has made me free from the law of sin and death.[6] Enable me, precious Father, to stand fast in the liberty you have given to me so that I will never again be entangled with the yoke of bondage to shame.[7] Thank you for your truth which has truly made me free.[8]

Because of your Word and the Gospel of Jesus Christ, I am not ashamed any longer, because I know whom I have believed.[9] I will not believe the lies and accusations of the devil any longer; in fact, I resist him in faith, and I know that he must flee from me.[10] Thank you, Father.

Keep on leading me as I study your Word of truth, because I know this will enable me to become a worker who never needs to experience shame, because I will know how to rightly divide your Word.[11] In Jesus' name I pray.[12] Thank you, Father.

References: *(1) Psalms 25:2; (2) 1 John 1:9; (3) 1 John 1:7; (4) 2 Corinthians 10:4; (5) Romans 8:1-2; (6) Romans 8:3; (7) Galatians 5:1; (8) John 8:32; (9) 2 Timothy 1:12; (10) James 4:7; (11) 2 Timothy 2:15; (12) John 15:16.*

104

SINGLE MOTHERHOOD

A Breakthrough Prayer for a Single Mother

Key Scripture: *"Train up a child in the way he should go, and when he is old he will not depart from it"* (Prov. 22:6, NKJV).

Prayer: Lord God, I come to you in the name of Jesus Christ my Lord, and I look to you as I face the demands, joys, and challenges of single motherhood. Father, you are so great, and greatly to be praised.[1] You are my God forever.[2]

As I call upon you, I know you are ministering to my every need — emotional, spiritual, physical, and financial. I will always glorify you.[3] Your promises are so beautiful to me. My help is in your name, O Lord God; you have made heaven and earth.[4]

Even though I sometimes feel lonely, I know you always hear my cry. You always attend to my prayer.[5] Thank you, Father. When my heart is overwhelmed, you always lead me to the rock that is higher than I.[6]

Thank you, Father, for my children. I realize that they are a wonderful heritage — a reward from your hands.[7] Thank you for your promise, Father, to be a parent to me and to my children.[8] Thank you for sharing the parental responsibilities with me, and for showing me how to be an effective parent. Thank you for being a part of my family, Father. I know you are protecting us,[9] providing for us,[10] and watching out for us.[11]

You, Lord God, are my helper, and I will not fear what others shall do unto me.[12] I thank you that you are the Giver of every good and perfect gift, and you never change.[13] I cast all my cares upon you, because I know you care for me.[14] Thank you, mighty God, for supplying all my needs, as well as the needs of every member of my family.[15]

Impart to me the wisdom and patience I need. I know you always give liberally to all who ask in faith.[16] Through faith, I ask for wisdom, Father.[17] I believe that you desire above all else that I should prosper and be in health even as my soul prospers.[18] Thank you, Father. I claim this promise for both me and my children.

Lord God, I trust you with all my heart. I choose not to lean unto my own understanding. Instead, I am determined to always lean on you, and to acknowledge you in all my ways. I thank you for the knowledge that you will direct my paths.[19]

References: *(1) Psalms 48:1; (2) Psalms 48:14; (3) Psalms 50:15; (4) Psalms 124:8; (5) Psalms 61:1-2; (6) Psalms 61:2; (7) Psalms 127:3; (8) Psalms 68:5; (9) Psalms 91; (10) Psalms 132:15; (11) Jeremiah 31:28; (12) Hebrews 13:6; (13) James 1:17; (14) 1 Peter 5:7; (15) Philippians 4:19; (16) James 1:4-5; (17) James 1:5-6; (18) 3 John 2; (19) Proverbs 3:5-6.*

105

SINGLE WOMANHOOD

A Breakthrough Prayer for a Single Woman

Key Scripture: *"Commit thy way unto the Lord; trust also in Him"* (Ps. 37:5).

Prayer: O God, my wonderful Father, I do commit my way unto you, and I will trust in you,[1] because you are the Lord of my life. Though some trust in chariots, and some in horses, I will remember your mighty name.[2] All my happiness comes from trusting you, Father.[3] Help me to trust you more fully, instead of leaning upon my own understanding. In all my ways I want to acknowledge you, Lord God, and I know you will direct my paths.[4] Thank you for your promise to direct me with regard to my career and all my relationships.

It is my heart's desire, Father, to do all to your glory.[5] It is my honor to serve the Lord Christ.[6] Whatever you give me to do, I will do it with all my heart.[7]

Lead me to the right friends — people who will love at all times. Help me to be such a friend to others as well, Father.[8] Help me to receive my fellow-believers as Christ received me, to your glory, Father.[9]

In times of loneliness and discouragement, help me to remember that you are with me, Father.[10]   In fact, you never leave me nor forsake me.[11]

Thank you, Lord God. I place my future in your hands, fully confident that you have a plan and a purpose for my life,[12] and you will weave all things together perfectly, because I love you.[13]

References: *(1) Psalms 37:5; (2) Psalms 20:7; (3) Proverbs 16:20; (4) Proverbs 3:5-6; (5) 1 Corinthians 10:31; (6) Colossians 3:24; (7) Ecclesiastes 9:10; (8) Proverbs 17:17; (9) Romans 15:7; (10) John 16:32; (11) Hebrews 13:5; (12) Jeremiah 29:11-13; (13) Romans 8:28.*

106

SINGLE WOMANHOOD

*A Breakthrough Prayer for a Woman
Who Desires a Mate*

Key Scripture: *"Therefore a man shall leave his
father and mother and be joined to his wife, and they
shall become one flesh"* (Gen. 2:24, NKJV).

Prayer: Father God, I come to you now in the
name of my wonderful Lord Jesus Christ. Thank
you for instituting marriage as your special
blessing and plan for your children. I have a
desire to be married, and I ask you for clear
guidance and wisdom in the choice of the man
that you have prepared to be my mate.[1] Lead me
in your perfect way[2] and in your perfect will.[3]

Prevent me, O Lord, from ever being
unequally yoked in any way with my future
husband.[4] I ask that you would lead my future
husband to a saving knowledge of your Son,
my Lord and Savior Jesus Christ.[5] Help him,
Father, to keep himself sexually pure from this
time forward and always.[6]

I pray, dear God, that I will be able to say,
"One man among a thousand have I found"[7]
because of his godly life, and because of his
tender love for and devotion to me. May he be a
man who loves your Word and realizes that I am
his glory and may he always honor me as your
daughter and as his wife.[8] I pray that he will love
me as Christ loves the Church,[9] and that he will

lay down his life in loving devotion to me.[10] May he always cherish and honor me as the weaker vessel and as being an heir together with him of the grace of life, so that his prayers may not be hindered.[11] May our love for each other and for you, Lord, be a witness to others as well.[12]

Pour your grace upon our marriage, Father, so that our marriage will be strong and filled with love and joy. May our marriage and family be a source of fulfillment and happiness for us throughout our lives.

May my future husband truly be a man of God who properly and wisely establishes his authority in our home under your direction.[13] May he ever rejoice in me as his wife.[14]

I pray also, Lord, that my husband and I will always walk in wise understanding of your will,[15] and that in righteousness and holiness we will submit ourselves to one another in the reverent fear of God.[16] Let your favor be great toward us,[17] and let us fulfill your joy by being faithful followers of God, as dear children, walking in love as Christ also loved us.[18]

References: (1) James 1:5; (2) Psalms 18:30; (3) Luke 11:2; (4) 2 Corinthians 6:14; (5) Ephesians 2:8-9; (6) 1 Timothy 5:22; (7) Ecclesiastes 7:28; (8) 1 Corinthians 11:7; (9) Ephesians 5:25; (10) John 15:13; (11) 1 Peter 3:7; (12) John 13:35; (13) Ephesians 5:23-24; (14) Proverbs 5:18; (15) Ephesians 5:17; (16) Ephesians 5:21; (17) Psalms 5:12; (18) Ephesians 5:2.

107

STRENGTH

*A Breakthrough Prayer for a Woman
Who Seeks Greater Strength*

Key Scripture: *"The joy of the Lord is your strength"* (Neh. 8:10).

Prayer: Almighty God, I seek your joy which is great strength to me.[1] You are my strength and song, dear Father.[2] You are my strength and my shield.[3] Your right hand, O Lord God, is glorious in power.[4] I claim your promise that I can do all things through Christ who strengthens me.[5]

Your ways are strength to me, Father.[6] In my weakness you perfect your strength.[7] Thank you, mighty Father. You, Lord God, are my strength,[8] and I will lean on your strength, not my own presumed ability, because I realize that it's not by might nor by power, but by your Spirit that I shall prevail.[9] Fill me with your Spirit, Father.[10]

Wisdom and might are yours.[11] Give me your wisdom,[12] and your strength.[13] I will trust in you forever, Lord God, because in you I have everlasting strength.[14] Thank you, Father.

Help me always to remember that the race is not to the swift, nor the battle to the strong,[15] but it is you, Lord God, my strength, who teaches my hands to war, and my fingers to fight.[16]

Thank you for being my strength and my song, for you, Lord God, have become my salvation.[17]

References: *(1) Nehemiah 8:10; (2) Exodus 15:2; (3) Psalms 28:7; (4) Exodus 15:6; (5) Philippians 4:13; (6) Proverbs 10:29; (7) 2 Corinthians 12:9; (8) Isaiah 49:5; (9) Zechariah 4:6; (10) Ephesians 5:18; (11) Daniel 2:20; (12) James 1:5; (13) Daniel 11:32; (14) Isaiah 26:4; (15) Ecclesiastes 9:11; (16) Psalms 144:1; (17) Psalms 118:14.*

108

STRONGHOLDS OF THE MIND

*A Breakthrough Prayer for a Woman Who Needs
to Have Her Mental Strongholds Demolished*

Key Scripture: *"Whosoever shall call on the name
of the Lord shall be delivered"* (Joel 2:32).

Prayer: Heavenly Father, certain mental
strongholds have prevented me from moving
on with you. I ask you to overthrow these
strongholds in the name of Jesus. Specifically,
I ask you to conquer the stronghold of _____

_____

in my life.

Though I walk in the flesh, dear Father, I
realize that I do not war according to the flesh.[1]
Therefore, I call upon you to deliver me from
the strongholds that threaten to undo me.[2]
Thank you for giving me the spiritual weapons
of your Word,[3] the blood of Jesus,[4] and the
word of my testimony[5] to conquer all forces of
evil in my life. I raise these weapons now in
the name of Jesus Christ.

Thank you for showing me that my
weapons are not carnal, but they are mighty in
you for the pulling down of this stronghold.[6]
Through your power, almighty God, I cast
down all arguments and every high thing that
exalts itself against knowing you, and I bring

every one of my thoughts into captivity to the obedience of Christ.[7]

Continue your work of deliverance in my life,[8] and help me to stand fast in the liberty you've given to me.[9] I put on all the armor you've given to me, Father, so that I will be able to stand against the wiles of the devil.[10] I take the shield of faith which I will use to quench all the fiery darts of the wicked one,[11] and I will wear the helmet of salvation to protect my mind at all times.[12] Help me always to wield the sword of your Spirit, which is your mighty Word,[13] and to pray always with all prayer and supplication in your Spirit.[14]

Now that I've sought you, and I know you've heard me, I realize that you have delivered me from the strongholds that held me back so long.[15] From this day forward I will be strong in you, Lord, and in the power of your might.[16] Thank you so much, O God.

References: (1) 2 Corinthians 10:3; (2) Psalms 71:2; (3) Hebrews 4:12; (4) Revelation 12:11; (5) Revelation 12:11; (6) 2 Corinthians 10:4; (7) 2 Corinthians 10:5; (8) Psalms 142:7; (9) Galatians 5:1; (10) Ephesians 6:11; (11) Ephesians 6:16; (12) Ephesians 6:17; (13) Ephesians 6:17; (14) Ephesians 6:18; (15) Daniel 6:27; (16) Ephesians 6:10.

109

STUDENT

*A Breakthrough Prayer of Academic Success
for a Woman in School*

Key Scripture: *"Hear instruction, and be wise,
and refuse it not"* (Prov. 8:33).

Prayer: Dear Father, give me now wisdom and knowledge[1] so that I will always be attentive to my studies and be wise.[2] Give me your peace, and teach me your wisdom.[3] As I continue in my studies, I will walk in peace, knowing that you will teach me your wisdom.[4] Thank you, Father.

As I commit my works unto you, O Lord, I know you will establish my thoughts.[5] As I walk in faith, I know you will establish and prosper me in all that I do.[6] As I continue to seek you, I know you will help me to be successful in all my endeavors.[7] Even in my studies, Lord God, I know that it is not by my might, nor by my power, but it's through your Spirit that I shall prevail.[8] Thank you, Father.

Help me, loving God, to commit all my academic responsibilities to you, to walk in faith, to always seek you, and to lean upon your power. I thank you for your power which always helps me.[9] I will accomplish my schoolwork unto your glory, Father.[10] Without you I can do nothing,[11] but through you I can do all things.[12]

Enable me to study effectively so that I will be able to show myself to be a student who never needs to be ashamed because I have learned how to rightly divide your Word.[13] Help me to walk in your Word at all times,[14] and to live according to the truth your Word imparts to me.[15]

Thank you, Lord God, for making me a successful student.

References: (1) Proverbs 2:7; (2) Proverbs 8:33; (3) Job 33:33; (4) Proverbs 2:7; (5) Proverbs 16:3; (6) Isaiah 7:9; (7) 2 Chronicles 26:5; (8) Zechariah 4:6; (9) 2 Chronicles 25:8; (10) 1 Corinthians 10:31; (11) John 15:5; (12) Philippians 4:13; (13) 2 Timothy 2:15; (14) Psalms 119:105; (15) Psalms 119:142.

110

SUICIDAL THOUGHTS

A Breakthrough Prayer for a Woman
Who Is Plagued by Thoughts of Committing Suicide

Key Scripture: *"And they overcame him by the blood of the Lamb and by the word of their testimony"* (Rev. 12:11, NKJV).

Prayer: O God, the depression I've been experiencing causes me to contemplate the idea of taking my own life, but I know this is not your will for me. Therefore, I come to you now, seeking your help to overcome this temptation of the enemy through the blood of Jesus Christ and the word of my testimony.[1]

Out of the depths I have cried to you, O Lord God![2] Hear my voice, and let your ears be attentive to the voice of my supplications.[3] Thank you for forgiving me of my sins.[4] I wait for you, Lord God. My soul waits, and in your Word do I hope.[5]

I praise you, God, for Jesus who came to set the captives free. He has given me authority over all the power of the enemy.[6] Through faith in your Word, I now resist the devil and all his lies, deceptions, and accusations concerning suicide, and I bring every thought and feeling captive to the obedience of Jesus Christ my Lord.[7] Thank you, Father, for delivering me from the power of darkness, and translating me into the kingdom of the Son of your love.[8]

I resist the spirit of suicide, and I will continue to do so, because I know that when I resist the devil he flees from me.[9] Give me clear insight regarding the deceptive thoughts of the enemy who comes to steal, kill, and destroy.[10] Help me always to remember that Jesus came to give me the more abundant life.[11]

My soul waits for you more than those that watch for the morning.[12] I find my hope in you, Father, because I know that with you there is mercy and abundant redemption.[13] In spite of my depression and despair, I will praise you with my whole heart.[14] I will worship toward your holy temple, and I will praise your name, Father, for your lovingkindness and truth. Thank you for magnifying your Word above your name.[15]

I know that you have heard my prayer, Father, and you are making me bold with strength in my soul.[16] Though I walk in the midst of trouble, I know you are reviving me, and you are stretching out your hand against the enemy. Thank you for the saving power of your right hand, Father.[17]

I claim your promise by faith that you will perfect that which concerns me, because I know that your mercy endures forever. Help me at all times to stand fast in the liberty with which you have set me free from all thoughts of suicide and to never again be entangled with that yoke of bondage.[18]

Thank you, Father, for delivering me.[19] I bless you now, and I will bless you at all times. Your praise shall be continually in my mouth. My soul will make its boast in you, O God, because I sought you, and you heard me, and you delivered me from all my fears. You saved me out of all my troubles.[20]

References: (1) *Revelation 12:11; (2) Psalms 130:1; (3) Psalms 130:2; (4) Psalms 130:4; (5) Psalms 130:5; (6) Luke 10:19; (7) 2 Corinthians 10:5; (8) Colossians 1:13; (9) James 4:7; (10) John 10:10; (11) John 10:10; (12) Psalms 130:6; (13) Psalms 130:7; (14) Psalms 138:1-2; (15) Psalms 138:2; (16) Psalms 138:3; (17) Psalms 138:7; (18) Galatians 5:1; (19) Psalms 34:17-18; (20) Psalms 34:1-6.*

111

TEMPTATION

A Breakthrough Prayer for a Woman
Who Wants to Overcome Temptation

Key Scripture: *"The Lord knows how to deliver the godly out of temptations"* (2 Pet. 2:9, NKJV).

Prayer: Almighty Father, thank you for your power which is able to deliver me out of all temptations.[1] I claim your power as I pray for your overcoming strength with regard to the temptation of _____.

How I thank you and praise you for the knowledge that the temptations I face are common to people everywhere. Father, I know you are faithful to me, and you will not allow me to be tempted beyond my ability to endure. I believe that with every temptation you will provide me with a way to escape that will enable me to endure it.[2] Thank you, Father.

Therefore, I submit myself to you, knowing that as I do so, when I resist the devil, he will flee from me.[3] Lead me not into temptation, and deliver me from evil, I pray,[4] as I watch and pray so as never to willingly enter into temptation.[5] I yield myself to you.[6]

It thrills me to know that as I learn to endure temptation, I can look forward to the crown of life that you have promised to all

those who love you, Father.[7] I also am very
thankful to know that you will never bring
temptation my way, Lord God. Thank you for
showing me that I am tempted when I am
drawn away by own lusts and desires, and I
am enticed.[8]   Keep me from ever being
deceived by this process again, dear Father,
because I know that conceived desire brings
forth sin, and sin brings forth death.[9]

In order to protect myself, therefore, I
now put on your perfect armor.[10] Thank you
for your helmet of salvation which protects my
mind,[11] for I am a new creation in Christ Jesus.[12]
Thank you for the breastplate of righteousness
which protects my heart.[13] And I especially
thank you for the sword of the Spirit (your holy
Word),[14] which I will boldly wield against the
enemy. Thank you, also, dear Father, for the
shield of faith which I will use to quench all the
fiery darts of temptation from the wicked one.[15]

Thank you for your promise to deliver me
from all temptation.

References: *(1) 2 Peter 2:9; (2) 1 Corinthians 10:13;*
(3) James 4:7; (4) Matthew 6:13; (5) Matthew 26:41;
(6) Romans 6:13; (7) James 1:12; (8) James 1:14;
(9) James 1:15; (10) Ephesians 6:10-11; (11) Ephesians
6:17; (12) 2 Corinthians 5:17; (13) Ephesians 6:14;
(14) Ephesians 6:17; (15) Ephesians 6:16.

112

TRUSTING GOD

A Breakthrough Prayer for a Woman
Who Wants to Trust God Fully

Key Scripture: *"The Lord is my rock, and my fortress, and my deliverer; my God, my strength, in whom I will trust"* (Ps. 18:2).

Prayer: Lord God, almighty Father, I trust in you. You are my rock, my fortress, my deliverer, my God, and my strength.[1] I choose to trust in you — with all my heart — instead of leaning unto my own understanding. In all my ways, I will acknowledge you, and I know that you will direct my paths.[2] Thank you for this truth, Father.

Your Word, O God, gives me the faith to trust you.[3] Your Word, O God, is forever settled in heaven.[4] You watch over your Word to perform it.[5] Your Word never returns unto you void. It always accomplishes your purposes.[6]

I commit my way to you, Lord God.[7] Because I have put my trust in you, I will not fear what others can do to me.[8] I will call upon you, and I know you will hear me.[9]

You are my trust, almighty God.[10] You are my hope.[11] I look unto you continually.[12] I have chosen to trust you, and I will remember your name, Lord God.[13] You are Jehovah-jireh, my Provider.[14]   You are Jehovah-shalom, my peace.[15]

My joy increases in direct proportion to my ability to trust you, Father. Let me ever shout for joy because I trust in you.[16] Thank you for the happiness that comes to me as I learn to walk in trust.[17]

References: (1) Psalms 18:2; (2) Proverbs 3:5-6; (3) Romans 10:17; (4) Psalms 119:89; (5) Jeremiah 1:12; (6) Isaiah 55:11; (7) Psalms 37:5; (8) Psalms 56:4; (9) Proverbs 15:29; (10) Psalms 115:9; (11) Jeremiah 17:7; (12) Micah 7:7; (13) Psalms 8:1,9; (14) Genesis 22:14; (15) Judges 6:24; (16) Psalms 5:11; (17) Psalms 40:4.*

113

TRUTH

*A Breakthrough Prayer for a Woman
Who Wants to Walk in Truth*

Key Scripture: *"Ye shall know the truth, and the truth shall make you free"* (John 8:32).

Prayer: O God, thank you for your truth, and thank you for allowing me to know your truth which has made me free.[1] Enable me to walk in your truth at all times, and to stand fast in the liberty it has brought to me so that I will never again be entangled with any yoke of bondage.[2]

Your Word is truth, heavenly Father,[3] and I love your Word with all my heart. Lead me and guide me so that I will walk in your Word at all times, for I know that your Word is a light unto my path and a lamp unto my feet.[4] Thank you, Father.

Thank you for sending Jesus who is the way, the truth, and the life for me,[5] and for sending your Holy Spirit who is the Spirit of truth.[6] I ask that the Holy Spirit would guide me into all truth.[7] Indeed, I thank you that the Spirit is truth.[8]

Lord God, I praise you for the fact that your truth endures to all generations.[9] Your Word contains the truth I need to walk in.[10] Your Word has been true from the beginning.[11]

I love your Word of truth,[12] and I rejoice in the fact that your words shall never pass away.[13]

Thank you for your truth, Father. From this time forth I will walk in your truth.

References: (1) John 8:32; (2) Galatians 5:1; (3) John 17:17; (4) Psalms 119:105; (5) John 14:6; (6) John 16:13; (7) John 16:13; (8) 1 John 5:6; (9) Psalms 100:5; (10) Psalms 119:142; (11) Psalms 119:160; (12) Zechariah 8:19; (13) Mark 13:31.

114

VICTORY

*A Breakthrough Prayer for a Woman
in Need of Victory*

Key Scripture: *"Thanks be to God, who gives
us the victory through our Lord Jesus Christ"*
(1 Cor. 15:57, NKJV).

Prayer: Father in heaven, how I thank you for
giving me the victory through my Lord Jesus
Christ.[1] The realization that He has overcome
the world truly fills my heart with joy.[2] Now I
know that because I've been born of you,
Father, I, like Jesus, shall be able to overcome
the world.[3]

Father, I thank you that my faith is the
victory that overcomes the world,[4] and I will
sing unto you because I know you have
triumphed gloriously.[5] Thank you, Father.

My need for victory in my life is most
evident in the following area: _____
_____.

I ask you, Father, to give me a breakthrough
of victory in this area because I know your
right hand is glorious in power.[6] Thank
you for fighting for me in this particular
battle.[7] Thank you for favoring me by
not letting my enemies triumph over me.[8]
Through faith, I am able to overcome the

devil through the blood of the Lamb and the word of my testimony.[9] Greater is He that is in me than he that is in the world.[10] In fact, I am more than a conqueror through Jesus Christ my Lord.[11] Thank you, Father.

Power belongs to you, almighty God.[12] There is no power but of you.[13] In light of all this truth, and in the mighty name of Jesus Christ,[14] I claim complete and total victory over _____

_____

to your glory, almighty Father.

References: *(1) 1 Corinthians 15:57; (2) John 16:33; (3) 1 John 5:4; (4) 1 John 5:4; (5) Exodus 15:1; (6) Exodus 15:6; (7) Joshua 23:10; (8) Psalms 41:11; (9) Revelation 12:11; (10) 1 John 4:4; (11) Romans 8:37; (12) Psalms 62:11; (13) Romans 13:1; (14) Acts 3:16.*

115

WEIGHT LOSS

*A Breakthrough Prayer for a Woman
Who Wants to Lose Weight*

Key Scripture: *"Beloved, I pray that you may prosper in all things and be in health, just as your soul prospers"* (3 John 2, NKJV).

Prayer: O Lord my God, I pray now in the name of my Lord Jesus Christ, and I thank you for showing me that you want me to walk in health and prosper even as my soul prospers.[1] Help me, I pray, to lose weight. I know that when I cry out to you, you bring health to me.[2] Thank you, Father.

Help me to maintain my body and weight by being very careful about what I eat and how much I eat. I realize that I am redeemed by the blood of my Lord and Savior Jesus Christ,[3] and I know that my body is the temple of the Holy Spirit. Therefore, I want to honor you with the way I treat the temple of my body,[4] especially by eating properly.

Father, empower me to profit through bodily exercise,[5] and good nutrition so that I will be able to serve you more fully and effectively. Through your grace, I will keep my heart merry because I know this will do me good.[6] Help me to keep my focus on things that are honest, true, just, pure, lovely, and of good report at all times[7] instead of on food and eating. Enable me to walk in your Spirit, Father, so that I will not fulfill the lust of the flesh,[8] and so that I might be able to bear the fruit of your Spirit in all my responsibilities and relationships.[9] I especially ask you to help me to walk in the fruit of self-control as I endeavor to practice positive principles of good health in my diet and physical exercise.[10]

I praise you, Father, for your promise of good health,[11] and I ask you to guide me in my dieting and nutrition. Thank you, Father, for giving me every herb and every tree with its fruit for my nourishment and health.[12] Help me to make wise choices about my eating habits each day.[13] I want Jesus to be Lord over every area of my life. Therefore, I now pray and declare that Jesus Christ is Lord over my eating habits and the appetites of my body.[14] I surrender completely to you, Lord Jesus. I rejoice that I can do all things through Christ who strengthens me.[15] I praise you, Lord, for the certain knowledge that you are giving me the victory in these areas, and you are helping me to lose weight.

References: *(1) 3 John 2; (2) Psalms 30:2; (3) Revelation 5:9; (4) 1 Corinthians 6:19-20; (5) 1 Timothy 4:8; (6) Proverbs 17:22; (7) Philippians 4:8; (8) Galatians 5:16; (9) Galatians 5:22-23; (10) Galatians 5:23; (11) Jeremiah 30:17; (12) Genesis 1:29; (13) James 1:5; (14) Philippians 2:11; (15) Philippians 4:13.*

116

WIDOWHOOD

*A Breakthrough Prayer for a Woman
Who Is a Widow*

Key Scripture: *"A Father of the fatherless, a defender of widows, is God in His holy habitation"* (Ps. 68:5, NKJV).

Prayer: Thank you, mighty Father, for being my defender.[1] I trust in you.[2] Help me to trust in you with all my heart, and not to lean unto my own understanding. In all my ways, dear God, I will acknowledge you, and I know you will direct my paths.[3] Thank you, Father.

You are my rock, mighty Father.[4] Thank you for not leaving me comfortless.[5] I praise you for being the Father of mercies, and the God of all comfort.[6] I will endeavor to keep my mind stayed on you and to trust you, because I know this gives me perfect peace.[7] Thank you, Father.

Your Holy Spirit is my precious Comforter.[8] I receive the comfort and ministry of the Holy Spirit in my life right now. Thank you for Him, Father. You are a shield for me. You are my glory, and the lifter of my head.[9]

I will not fear any longer, Father, because I know you are with me.[10] Thank you for your promise to never leave me nor forsake me.[11]

I receive your peace,[12] joy,[13] and love[14] now as I pray. I thank you for my Lord Jesus Christ through whom I may come boldly to your throne of grace where I always obtain mercy and grace to help me in my times of need.[15]

O God, you are my wonderful Father.

References: (1) Psalms 68:5; (2) Jeremiah 49:11; (3) Proverbs 3:5-6; (4) Psalms 42:9; (5) John 14:18; (6) 2 Corinthians 1:3; (7) Isaiah 26:3; (8) John 14:16; (9) Psalms 3:3; (10) Genesis 26:24; (11) Hebrews 13:5; (12) Psalms 119:165; (13) Nehemiah 8:10; (14) Romans 5:8; (15) Hebrews 4:16.

117

WISDOM

A Breakthrough Prayer for a Woman
Who Wants to Walk in Wisdom

Key Scripture: *"The Lord giveth wisdom: out of His mouth cometh knowledge and understanding"* (Prov. 2:6).

Prayer: Lord God, thank you for the wisdom you impart to me through your Word. I ask for more of your knowledge, understanding, and wisdom.[1] Thank you for your Word which tells me that if I lack wisdom I may simply ask of you, because you give wisdom liberally to all who ask, believing. I claim the promise of your Word which tells me that your wisdom will be imparted unto me.[2] It is with great faith that I seek your wisdom, without any doubting.[3]

Give me wisdom and knowledge now, I pray.[4] Father, I want to walk in your wisdom because I realize its price is above rubies.[5] I hold my peace, dear God, and as I do so, I know you are imparting greater wisdom unto me.[6]

I thank you, Father, that as I walk in your wisdom I experience pleasantness in my life,[7] and your wisdom is a tree of life to me.[8] I will not forsake the wisdom you give to me, because I know it will preserve me. In fact, I will always love your wisdom, and as I do so, I know it shall keep me.[9]

Because wisdom is the principal thing, I will seek it with all my heart,[10] and I will always endeavor to walk in it. Wisdom is my sister, and understanding is my kinswoman.[11] Thank you, Father-God, for the life your wisdom imparts to me.[12]

Your glorious wisdom strengthens me,[13] and it makes my face to shine.[14] Your wisdom is better than strength,[15] and better than the weapons of war.[16] I thank you, Father, that wisdom and might are yours,[17] and that you always desire to impart them to me.

References: (1) Proverbs 2:6; (2) James 1:5; (3) James 1:6; (4) 2 Chronicles 1:10; (5) Job 28:18; (6) Job 33:33; (7) Proverbs 3:17; (8) Proverbs 3:18; (9) Proverbs 4:6; (10) Proverbs 4:7; (11) Proverbs 7:4; (12) Proverbs 8:35; (13) Ecclesiastes 7:19; (14) Ecclesiastes 8:1; (15) Ecclesiastes 9:16; (16) Ecclesiastes 9:18; (17) Daniel 2:20.

118

WORKING WOMAN

A Breakthrough Prayer for a Working Woman

Key Scripture: *"Commit thy works unto the Lord, and thy thoughts shall be established"* (Prov. 16:3).

Prayer: Father-God, I commit my work and my career unto you, and I thank you for your promise to establish my thoughts.[1] I rejoice before you, Lord God, in all the work that I have to do.[2] Thank you for giving me this job. Help me to be a faithful worker.

I will not let your Word depart from my mouth. I will meditate in your Word day and night, and I will observe to do according to all that is written in it. In this way I know you will make my way prosperous, and you will grant me good success.[3] Thank you, Father. I ask for your favor,[4] prosperity,[5] your guidance,[6] and your wisdom.[7] Encompass me with your favor like a shield, mighty God.[8]

My delight is in your Word, and as I meditate in your Word both day and night, I shall become like a fruitful tree that is planted by the water. My leaf shall not wither, and whatever I do shall prosper.[9] Thank you for the precious promises of your Word, Father.

Help me to do my work with all my might,[10] realizing, mighty God, that I am a co-laborer with you.[11] Thank you for the promise of rest you give to me through Jesus Christ who invites me to come unto Him when I am hard at work and heavy burdened so that He can give me rest.[12] I receive His promise, and purpose to work in an attitude of rest.

Empower me to do everything that I do unto your glory, Father.[13] I serve the Lord Jesus Christ,[14] and I know I shall receive the reward of your inheritance.[15] It is my desire, dear Father, to study your Word faithfully so that I will be a worker who never needs to be ashamed because I know how to rightly divide your Word.[16]

Help me to be subject to those you have put over me in the workplace,[17] because I realize that those in authority are ordained of you, Father, and you desire me to be subject unto them.[18] Enable me to maintain a good attitude toward my employers, my fellow-employees, and my job at all times. Help me, also, dear Father, to be thankful in everything I do, because I know this is your will for me.[19]

References: *(1) Proverbs 16:3; (2) Deuteronomy 12:18; (3) Joshua 1:8; (4) Proverbs 3:4; (5) 3 John 2; (6) Psalms 73:24; (7) James 1:5; (8) Psalms 5:12; (9) Psalms 1:1-4; (10) Ecclesiastes 9:10; (11) 1 Corinthians 3:9; (12) Matthew 11:28; (13) 1 Corinthians 10:31; (14) Colossians 3:24; (15) Colossians 3:24; (16) 2 Timothy 2:15; (17) Romans 13:1; (18) Romans 13:1; (19) 1 Thessalonians 5:18.*

119

WORRY

*A Breakthrough Prayer for a Woman
Who Wants Freedom From Worry*

Key Scripture: *"Therefore humble yourselves
under the mighty hand of God, that He may exalt
you in due time, casting all your care upon Him, for
He cares for you"* (1 Pet. 5:6-7, NKJV).

Prayer: God, I come to you because I know I
need freedom from worry. Therefore, I humble
myself under your mighty hand as I cast all my
cares upon you, because I know you do care
for me.[1] Thank you, Father. As I cast my
burdens upon you, I know you will sustain
me.[2] As I pour out my heart before you, I realize
what a wonderful refuge you are for me.[3]

Father, help me to be sober and vigilant,
because I realize that my adversary, the devil,
walks about like a roaring lion, seeking whom
he may devour.[4] All too often, he has tried to
devour me through worry, and, with your help,
I will resist him, steadfast in the faith.[5] You are
the God of all grace, and I thank you for calling
me to your eternal glory by Jesus Christ. I ask
that you would perfect, establish, strengthen,
and settle me.[6] Thank you, Father.

Realizing that at times the cares of this
world and the worries I've experienced, have

choked out your Word in my life,[7] I pledge to you that I will walk in the light your Word provides to me. Thank you for your Word which is a light unto my path and a lamp unto my feet.[8] Thank you, also, for Jesus who has given me a peace that the world can't give and can't take away from me.[9] I will keep my mind stayed upon you, Father, as I continue to trust in you, because I realize that this is the source of perfect peace in my life.[10]

I will be anxious for nothing, but in everything by prayer and supplication, with thanksgiving, I will let my requests be made known to you, and your peace, which surpasses all understanding, will guard my heart and mind through Christ Jesus.[11]

Thank you for giving me complete freedom from worry. Help me to stand fast in the liberty you've given unto me so that I will never again be entangled with the yoke of bondage that worry has imposed upon me.[12]

References: *(1) 1 Peter 5:7; (2) Psalms 55:22; (3) Psalms 62:8; (4) 1 Peter 5:8; (5) 1 Peter 5:9; (6) 1 Peter 5:10; (7) Matthew 13:22; (8) Psalms 119:105; (9) John 14:27; (10) Isaiah 26:3; (11) Philippians 4:6-7; (12) Galatians 5:1.*

Up date the New Spirit filled bible in
SEPTEMBER   NELSON BIBLE
                   SAMUEL

BOOK.
FRANKLIN GRAHM < Billy graham SON

ROL Hale
14171 Chorbour
TUSTIN CA 92713
CHURCH CH

W W W. T BN, ORg TBN.